New Life Hacks

1200+ Collection of Amazing Life Hacks

By Ravi Jain

Disclaimer:
This book is published after
a thorough research of the
Life Hacks. If you have
any suggestion for this book
to make it more interesting
please review or contact the author.
We will love to hear from you.

E-Mail: Jain.ravi002@gmail.com

Twitter: twitter.com/jainravi002

Table of Content

Introduction

Life hack (or life hacking) refers to any trick, shortcut, skill, or novelty method that increases productivity and efficiency, in all walks of life. The term was primarily used by computer experts who suffer from information overload or those with a playful curiosity in the ways they can accelerate their workflow in ways other than programming.

Ravi Jain

Brainy

1. Make a password into a goal of yours so you constantly have to be reminded of it.

2. When starting a game of "rock paper scissors" always start with paper. Most people start with rock as it's the shape the hand easily forms.

3. Fold your receipt around the gift card to always know your balance.

4. If you are buying headphones/speakers, test them with Bohemian Rhapsody. It has the complete set of highs and lows in instruments and vocals.

5. Rhythm", "zephyr", and "sphynx" are the three best possible hangman words.

6. Want to meet girls? Go outside when it's raining with a huge umbrella and take your pick.

7. If your area is ever below 32 degrees this winter, go outside and blow bubbles! They instantly turn to ice!

8. Music is so influential on the brain that the type you listen to actually has the ability to change the way you think and look at the world.

9. If you chew gum when you study a subject and then chew the same flavor when you the take the test it can help you remember.

10. Want to find a job after college? Be friends with as many people as possible in your field but on pace to graduate 1-2 years ahead of you.

11. Have a problem with not remembering if you took your pills or not? Flip the bottle every time you take them.

12. Don't want the person you are calling to know that it's you? Dial *67 before the number and he/she won't have a clue.

13. Need to test a printer? Print the Google homepage, it has all the colors and uses almost no ink.

14. If you're giving a big presentation, have a friend ask you a set question. This way, you'll look like you know your stuff really well.

15. If there's an annoying customer behind you in the checkout line, you can press all four corners of the credit card machine to have it reset.

16. The Two-Minute Rule: If you see something that needs doing, and it can be completed within two minutes, do it immediately.

17. Didn't finish your paper? Copy and paste a bunch of random symbols in a Word document and send it. Your teacher will think the file was damaged.

18. Secretaries, tech support and janitors are the true power in an office. Make friends; remember birthdays and you can get anything you need!

19. Don't burn yourself in those hard to reach candles, light a stick of spaghetti and light the wick with that.

20. Use a spring from an old pen to keep your charger from bending or breaking.

21. Suspect someone's giving you the wrong phone number? Read it back to them incorrectly, if they correct you, it's legit.

22. Keep a piece of paper and pencil by your bed. People mostly get their best ideas at night.

23. If you lose something in your room, take a picture of your room, put it on Facebook and have friends play "I spy".

24. When throwing a punch, clench your fist only at the last second. You lose a lot of power clenching throughout the swing.

25. Don't have a coin to flip? Look at the time. If it's even; heads. If it's odd; tails.

26. Mess with annoying telemarketers! Some aren't allowed to hang up, so answer the call, take a shower, have a snack, then say "no thanks".

27. Need to tell a believable lie? Include an embarrassing detail nobody doubts a story that makes you look dumb.

28. Respect your parents. They passed school without Google!

29. When buying something online only read the reviews that gave it 3 stars—they're usually the most honest about pros and cons.

30. Taking notes on the computer? Use a weird font. Studies have shown the uniqueness will make you more likely to remember them!

31. Start your day by thinking positive thoughts and you will have a positive day.

32. There are two rules to success... 1. Never reveal everything you know

33. Taking a quick nap after learning something new can solidify that memory in your brain.

34. Buy a world map shower curtain. You will become a geography expert from all the time you spend in the bathroom!

35. How to make "cheating" dice: Set oven to 250°, lay on cookie sheet w/ number you want to always face up when rolled, and cook for 10 minutes.

36. Sprinkle salt on a napkin before putting a drink on it to prevent the drink from sticking.

37. If you call your cable company and say you want more paid channels but haven't decided which ones, they might give you a free month of them all!

38. You can clear a room full of cigarette smoke in about a minute simply by spinning a wet towel around.

39. When proofreading, read out loud to yourself. Your mouth will catch errors your mind might glance over.

40. Music with a strong beat can stimulate brain waves which improve concentration, even after you've stopped listening.

41. Don't delay acting on a good idea. Chances are someone else has thought of it too. Success comes to the one who acts first.

42. Flip a Pizza box around on your lap so when opened the lid covers your chest... BOOM perfect Pizza Bib.

43. Have a good 20-minute workout in the morning. Then you can be lazy for the rest of the day, and you won't feel guilty!

44. Playing Tetris can increase brain power by almost 150%

45. When buying a romantic card, get two. Write the inscription from card A into card B and pretend you can write sweet things.

46. A high GPA looks good on paper, but networking and building friendships is what gets you a job.

47. Put a sticker with a fake PIN number on your debit card. If you lose it and someone tries to use it 3+ times, the machine will eat the card.

48. Solve "spot the difference" puzzles instantly by crossing your eyes. The differences will appear immediately.

49. Think of being with someone you like/love the moment before you get your picture taken... perfect natural smiles every time.

50. Take a picture of your fridge on your phone, you'll never struggle to remember what you need to buy at the grocery store!

51. Put that you were Time's 2006 person of the year on your resume/CV. In 2006, Time made "Everyone" the person of the year.

52. You can remember the value of pi (3.1415926) by counting each word's letters in "May I have a large container of coffee

53. Need to give CPR? Compress their chest hard to the beat of "Stayin' Alive" by the Bee Gees, the tempo is the correct timing of compressions.

54. SelfControl is a program that blocks sites like Facebook, Twitter and email for a specified period of time. So you can minimize distractions while you study/do homework.

55. Take notes on your professor's political ideologies and use this to your advantage when writing essays.

56. Take note of your body's sleeping position in the morning. This is probably your most comfortable sleeping position. Knowing this can help you get to sleep quicker!

57. Want to learn something? Try arguing with yourself. Conceiving opposition views leads to a more extensive examination of issue/topic.

58. Learning a new language? Try to find a translation of your favorite book when you were 9-12.

59. If you drop an earring, ring, or small screw simply turn off the lights and look with a flashlight. They'll light right up.

60. You can predict your future adult height with almost 100% accuracy by doubling your height at age two.

61. Want to know if someone has romantic feelings for you? Look at their eyes! People's pupils expand by 45% when looking at a love interest.

62. Eating chocolate while studying will help the brain retain new information more easily, and has been directly linked to higher test scores.

63. Before he even speaks, the way a man stands (slouching or not) accounts for 80% of a woman's first impression.

64. Ever hear a song on TV but you don't know what it is? WhatIsThatSong.net will tell you.

65. Playing a musical instrument has been known to raise a person's I.Q. by as much as 5 points.

66. If you ever go to a zoo, wear the same colors as the employees do. The animals will come right up to you instead of backing away.

67. When leaving heavy/bulky items in your shopping cart, position them with the bar codes facing up. The cashier will really appreciate it.

68. If someone is tailgating you turn on your windshield wiper fluid. It'll fly back and squirt them.

69. For girls: use your hair conditioner to shave your legs. It's a lot cheaper than shaving cream and leaves your legs really smooth.

70. Smile before answering the phone. It will make you sound happier and lead to a better conversation.

71. Tell people to pick a number between 12 and 5; 95% of people choose 7 (because they automatically subtract it).

72. Lending someone your pen? Keep the cap. No one accidentally keeps a pen without the cap.

73. Get a puppy before you decide to have children!

74. Life begins outside your comfort zone.

75. It's actually better to take exams on an empty stomach because hunger makes you focus better.

76. Got a flat tire? Take a picture of it on your phone. For future reference, you can text that picture to people as a great excuse!

77. Shoes smell like crap? Use dryer sheets as an incredibly effective shoe deodorizer.

78. Shoes smell bad? Put them in the freezer overnight. It will kill the bacteria and get rid of the stink.

79. Want to park somewhere you're not allowed to park? Keep the envelope from a parking ticket & put it under your windshield wipers.

80. Looking for something? Scan right to left with your eyes. You'll pick up more since your brain isn't used to reading that way.

81. When you have kids, watch the movie '2012' with them. Tell them that you survived that.

82. Create a phone contact called "ignore" and make the ringtone of that contact silent. Add in whoever you don't want to talk to.

83. When you blow out candles and they smoke, that smoke is actually wax. If you light the smoke quick enough it will spark the candle back up.

84. If you have a sore throat try eating a piece of cucumber. It cools down your throat and stops the itching.

85. Instead of using chemicals to fix your face complexion, drink a fruit smoothie every day with original Greek yogurt.

86. A clothed snowman melts slowly than a naked one!

87. If you ever need to stop and ask for directions, skip the gas station and find a pizza delivery place. They know their way around town!

88. Ask yourself if what you are doing today is getting you closer to where you want to be tomorrow.

89. When doing your nails, use Elmer's glue around your nail, let it dry, go crazy with paint and then peel off the glue.

90. If you get yourself to be really happy and excited to see other people, they will react the same to you. It doesn't always happen the first time, but it will definitely happen next time.

91. Before you diagnose yourself with depression or low self-esteem, first make sure that you are not, in fact, just surrounded by demotivating and irritating people.

92. Playing with puppies and kittens relieves stress and can help students perform better in exams.

93. To make someone think about something, tell them you do not want them to think about the it.

94. When signing up for a website, don't answer the security questions honestly. Always use the same wrong answer for max security.

95. Apply a generous amount of crushed aspirin onto a wart. Cover the wart with duct tape. The wart will disappear.

96. If you're having trouble making an important decision, sleep on it. Every big decision deserves at least 24 hours of consideration.

97. Taking notes? According to science you should write them by hands instead of using electronics to remember for longer periods.

98. Memorizing songs is extremely healthy for your brain and will improve your mental capacity.

99. Put your nail polish in the fridge for 15 minutes before you apply it as it goes on smoother.

100. When delivering your next speech print the speech and change the text color after every four lines. It makes it a lot easier while reading it.

101. Natural music to boost your productivity:
1. RainyMood.com
2. https://endlessvideo.com/watch?v=HMnrlotmd3k
3.https://endlessvideo.com/watch?v=DIx3aMRDUL4
.
Open all these three links together in three tabs.
Thank us later ;)

102. A woman's brain shrinks during the time of pregnancy, and it can take up to 6 months to regain the actual size.

103. Can using deodorant give you breast cancer? This myth has shed off as there is no conclusive evidence that using aluminium- or paraben containing deodorant can increase the risk for breast cancer.

104. Show some patience while taking your pet to the vet. They completely rely on research and testing. Plus, their patients can't even talk about the symptoms they are facing!

105. It costs $0 to be humble and kind!

106. It's a myth that all processed foods are bad. For real, both the ramen noodles and ready-to-serve brown rice are processed and have different nutritional values.

107. Go to sleep right after studying to remember and retain the information more effectively.

108. Whenever you are planning to start something new, Google search for "Things I wish I knew when I started XYZ." You will have a complete insight of it.

109. 70% of the women feel depressed after looking at a fashion magazine for 3 minutes. Be confident about yourself, don't fall for it.

Daily Life Solutions

1. If a bird ever gets into your house turn off all of the lights and open a door/window outside where there is visible light.

2. Wrinkly shirt? Throw it in the dryer with a few ice cubes for 5 minutes. Wrinkles gone!

3. Turn on your passenger seat warmer to keep food hot while driving home.

4. Best way to clean your microwave: Put a cup of hot water + vinegar inside, turn it on for 3-5 minutes. Wipe clean easily!

5. If you bought new jeans and they turn your hands blue, you can wash them with a tablespoon of salt to set the dye.

6. Do not use chemicals to kill ants. Instead, get a spray bottle, fill it with water and salt (25%), shake well, spray... boom, dead!

7. Nothing kills weeds and keeps them dead for longer like white vinegar straight from the bottle.

8. If a shirt/sweater has static cling, put a safety pin in it. The static will instantly go away.

9. Febreze kills ants on contact and doesn't leave your house smelling like poison.

10. Put two caps of pure Vanilla extract then place it in the oven for an hour. Within 20 minutes your house will smell like heaven!

11. How to make your own paint: mix 1 cup of salt, 1 cup of flour, 1 cup of water and food coloring.

12. In areas with lots of stoplights, going exactly the speed limit will help you hit more green lights.

13. Gum stuck to clothes. Boil vinegar, and pour on gum. Use a brush to wipe off. Gum will come off instantly.

14. If you eat enough blue M & Ms you can temporarily turn your skin a shade of light blue.

15. Spiders hate peppermint oil. Put some in a squirt bottle with water, spray your garage and all door frames, then watch the spiders run!

16. Holding a baby? Raise your eyebrows, don't furrow them. Babies are observant of faces, so they'll be less likely to cry.

17. Dip the top of your keys in paint to easily differentiate them.

18. When playing rock/paper/scissors, women are more likely to play scissors and men are more likely to play rock.

19. When a bag of chips is stuck in a vending machine, don't buy the same bag again to unjam it, buy something above it.

20. Before frying, sprinkle a little salt in your pan which will help keep the oil from splattering.

21. Don't wet your toothbrush after you put toothpaste. Water will reduce the Health & Fitness benefits of the toothpaste.

22. If you peel a banana from the bottom, you won't have to pick the little "stringy things" off of it.

23. Protuber is a free YouTube app on the iPhone which allows you to multitask while playing a video

24. Put dry tea bags in your smelly shoes or gym bags, it will absorb the unpleasant odor.

25. You can unroll the rim of Ketchup cups to increase their capacity.

26. Want whiter teeth? Gently rub the inside of a Banana peel around your teeth for two minutes, the minerals will absorb into your teeth and whiten them!

27. Toothpaste removes ink from your clothes. Apply it to the stain, let it dry and then wash.

28. Measure the length of your hand from the end of your palm to the top of your middle finger. Memorize it. Now you can judge the size of anything without a ruler.

29. Turn your steering wheel 180 degrees before parking in the sun. This way, you won't burn your hands when you start driving.

30. Dent in a ping pong ball? Hold a lighter under it (not too close or it'll burn) and the gasses expand, making it good as new.

31. Stick a paperclip to the end of a tape roll so you can always find where it starts.

32. If you want to amplify the sound from your smartphone when you're listening to music put it in a plastic solo cup.

33. Eating meat and dairy products increases your body's production of melanin; the compound that can help you stay tan in the winter months.

34. Baking soda catalyzes Superglue. A light sprinkle will cause even a large amount to set in seconds!

35. If you're pulling an all nighter, have a 15-20 minute nap just before the sun comes up and your body will reset itself.

36. Put 20 oz bottle caps under your Xbox 360 and PS3 so they get proper airflow on all six sides.

37. Always exhale when your left foot hits the ground to avoid cramps while running.

38. When heating leftovers, space out a circle in the middle, it will heat up much more evenly.

39. Whenever you make a packing list for a trip, make TWO copies, and use the second one to make sure you bring everything back.

40. If it's hot out and you just walked your dog, try giving him an ice cube/ice chips instead of water. He'll get both a cold drink as it melts, and a fun toy to play with!

41. Have flies in your house? They will follow bright lights, use this to guide them out windows.

42. Trying to quit smoking? Lick a little salt with the tip of your tongue whenever you feel the urge to smoke. This is said to break the habit within a month.

43. Pump up the volume on your iPhone/iPod by putting it in a bowl, the concave shape amplifies the music!

44. Cut slits in your corn dogs to stuff them with condiments!

45. Use toothpaste to clear up hazy car headlights. It works like a charm.

46. Before you marry someone you should first make them use a computer with super slow internet access to see who they truly are.

47. If you ever want to call a family meeting, just turn off the WiFi router and wait in the room in which its located.

48. When making cookies, replace butter with avocado. It tastes no different and makes the cookies surprisingly healthy for you.

49. Feeling too hot? Run your wrist under a cold tap for at least five minutes. It'll cool your blood down.

50. Want to watch a movie with a girl? Ask her what her favorite movie is and say you haven't seen it. She'll always say, "we have to watch it

51. Want to make sure you wake up in the morning? The Snooze App for iphone will donate to charity each time you hit the snooze button!

52. To remove gum from hair, dip into a small bowl of Coke, leave for a few minutes. The gum will wipe off.

53. When camping, use "joke candles" (the ones that can't get blown out) to light fires. This way, the wind won't affect the flame.

54. Take pictures of friends holding items you've lent them with your phone, so you remember down the road.

55. Don't know whether to write "affect" or "effect"? Use "impact" instead.

56. When limited water is available, rinse your mouth for 30 seconds before swallowing since most of your 'thirst' comes from a dry mouth.

57. If an image is burned into your plasma TV screen turn on static for about a day. Most of the time the image will fade away.

58. If you're ever attacked by a brown bear, play dead. If it's a black bear, punch it in the nose. It will run away.

59. A bit of toothpaste can successfully fix a scratched cell phone screen.

60. Holiday drink: Freeze coffee as ice cubes and toss in a cup of Baileys and Vanilla Vodka.

61. Instead of hitting backspace multiple times to correct misspelled words in windows, erase the whole word by pressing CTRL + BACKSPACE.

62. Drinking watermelon juice before a workout helps reduce muscle soreness.

63. If the disk is skipping, rub a banana over it to seal the minor scratches. Remember to wipe it off before you stick it back in.

64. When throwing a frisbee, use the same arm motion as if you were whipping a towel. This will ensure a straight throw every time.

65. To make a bruise go away, eat pineapple and papaya. They contain a digestive enzyme called bromelain that breaks down the proteins that can trap blood and fluids in your tissues. Eat as much pineapple as you want to flush away the bruise.

66. Need to cram for a test last minute? Your best chance of passing is to study the first and last 20% of the syllabus.

67. Trying to eat less? Use a smaller plate. It helps your mind think there's more food, and it limits what you can pile onto your plate.

68. Something in your eye? Hold your eyelashes and pull your eyelid down with your fingers, then blink rapidly several times.

69. Flattened pillow? Put it in the sun for 30 minutes. The sun will absorb moisture and plump up your pillow.

70. When boiling water and it starts foaming over, pour in some olive oil. Just a bit. It'll make the overflowing go away.

71. Getting nauseous from reading in a car? Tilt your head side to side and it'll go away!

72. Chalk will remove all grease stains. Simply rub the stain with chalk and toss it in the wash as normal.

73. When you get an email or text that infuriates you, wait about an hour to respond. You'll be surprised at how much more rational you become.

74. iPhone pictures will be better quality if you take the picture and then zoom in instead of zooming in to take the picture.

75. Put toilet paper in the toilet before using a public restroom to prevent loud splashing and backsplash.

76. Put 3 different Kool-aid ice cubes in a drink, add sprite and one or two shots of Vodka. The flavour of the drink will change as the ice melts.

77. To cry on command, relax your eyes for about 30 seconds. Then, gently rub them for about 10 seconds. Keep them open and tears will flow.

78. Have an infant? sleep with its baby blanket for one night. The result will be your smell on the blanket, which will help comfort

79. If you have sensitive ears, put Vaseline on earrings before putting them in. This will eliminate irritations.

80. If you buy unnecessary things that are on sale, you're not saving money, you are still spending.

81. Got stains on your sneakers? Scrub it with nail polish and they'll come right out.

82. Put your wet sponge in the microwave for 2 minutes to kill 99% of the bacteria.

83. Bad handwriting? Keep this in mind: more intelligent people tend to think faster, and as a result, their handwriting is more sloppy.

84. Googling a computer problem? Add "solved" to the search query to find the answer much faster.

85. Always clean your suitcases after staying in a hotel. Bed bugs often make the journey from the hotel room to your home via your suitcase.

86. Gum on your shoe? Spray it with some WD-40 and it'll come right off.

87. Tape a toy snake to the top of your car when you park and birds won't poop on it!

88. Ever have that thing in the back of your throat that makes you want to gag and cough it out? Scratch your ear, it will go away!

89. To speed the flow of ketchup out of a glass bottle, insert a drinking straw into it.

90. If you ever have to clean up vomit (and hopefully you don't), put ground coffee on it first. It takes away the smell and dehydrates it. You can then sweep it up easily.

91. Drilling small holes in the lower side of a garbage can make putting in and taking out bags much easier. No suction issues!

92. Keep apple slices from browning by holding them back together with rubber bands

93. Use a blow dryer to instantly defog any mirror.

94. If you're up late doing homework, listen to Hans Zimmer's Pandora. Music has no distracting lyrics, and the scores are intended to motivate.

95. Studies show that, if consumed in MODERATION, drinking tequila can actually significantly lower your risk for dementia.

96. Don't avoid cameras during your years in school or on vacation/holiday. You might not want to now, but you'll appreciate it later.

97. When a group of people laugh, people will instinctively look at the person they feel closest to in that group.

98. If your calculator runs out of batteries in the middle of an exam, rubbing the ends of the batteries together can give you an extra 15 mins.

99. Soak a cotton ball in vinegar and put it on a bruise to make it disappear!

100. 11 Stress Relieving Foods - Bananas - Pasta - Almonds - Grapes - Green Tea - Oatmeal - Chocolate - Watermelon - Orange Juice - Corn Flakes - Tuna.

101. Take a picture of yourself when your hair looks good. Show it to the barber next time you get a haircut. Perfect hair every time!

102. It's recommended that you use a 50-50 mixture of coolant and water in the car radiators, which helps in maintaining the anti-freeze level.

103. Pee shy? Start multiplying random numbers in your head. The same part of the brain controls both tasks and will help you get it started.

104. To instantly untangle headphones, pick a point about halfway along the wire and shake it.

105. Remove a splinter easily by applying a paste of baking soda and water, then waiting several minutes for the splinter to pop out of the skin.

106. If someone tells you they had a crush on you in high school, they usually still do.

107. On vending machines, if you press the buttons in the order 4, 2, 3, 1, you can sometimes get free drinks! Try it out.

108. Take a picture of business cards people hand you, just incase you lose them.

109. To quickly peel garlic, put it in a jar and shake well.

110. Put your eyeliner in the freezer for 5-10 minutes to prevent it from crumbling when you try to sharpen it.

111. Retractable pen (click pens) 'springs' works great to hold all your cards along at one place.

112. Walk away from anything or anyone who takes away joy from you. Life is too short to put up with fools.

113. If you're in an area where you should have cell phone service but don't, put your phone on airplane mode and then switch back. This will cause your phone to register and find all the towers in your vicinity.

114. Get a splinter? Pour a small amount of white glue on the area. Let it dry completely and peel it off. The splinter will come right out. Perfect method for children!

115. When finding it difficult to find someone a perfect gift, get a combination of 3 small gifts; one serious, one jokey and the last, homemade.

116. Want to sharpen blunt scissors? Cut through aluminium foils using them.

117. You can dust using a damp cloth to prevent dust from flying around.

118. Have a greasy stove filter? Empty a bottle of coca-cola on it, let it sit for 20 mins and brush it off. Rinse it with water and experience great filtration.

119. Always use shampoo in your windshield washer fluid in winters for better visibility during fog.

120. Rubbing up a walnut can help to cover up the dings on a damaged wooden furniture.

121. Zipper got stuck? Soap or window cleaner can make it move.

122. Use toothpaste instead of glue or screw to hang poster without making a hole on the wall. It will stick the poster to the wall and won't leave any bad sticky residue.

123. If chewing gum got stuck in your hair, don't panic and find ice cubes. By clamping the gum between two ice cubes for a minute will freeze the gum and make that structure more rigid to be scraped away.

124. Etsy.com, is an online platform where you can find hand crafted gift items at cheap prices!

125. Let go off all the rust deposited on your bathroom taps with tomato ketchup. Let it sit for 15 minutes and then wipe it off!

126. Bananas can reduce the swelling and irritation of mosquito bites and help with nicotine withdrawal.

127. Got a pimple before something important? Use an ice cube to shrink it!

128. If YouTube is forcing you to sign in, delete everything after the last / until you get to v= and then change v= to v/

129. To clean up vomit, put some ground coffee on it. It will take away the smell and dehydrate the vomit.

130. Remove the stains of oil from clothes by dabbing some white chalk over it.

131. Always give consideration to what your first instinct is telling you. Most of the times, it's right.

132. Use a fork and screw to uncork a bottle.

133. Get thicker eyelashes in 4-5 weeks with coconut oil. Put 2 tablespoons of coconut oil in a bowl and add 2 drops of lavender essential oil. Mix them well and your eyelash serum is ready!

134. Prevent your skirt from sticking to your legs by spraying the inside of a skirt with some hairspray. In case you're wearing tights underneath your skirt, spray your tights as well.

135. Ran out of shaving cream? Use olive oil for similar results.

136. Get rid of odours residing in your refrigerator by soaking a cotton ball or a sponge in lemon juice and placing it in the refrigerator.

137. Remove the stains of paint from clothes with (aerosol) hairspray. After applying a huge amount of spray, use a hard bristle scrubber and it will not deteriorate the quality of the cloth.

138. To clean your white, not-white-now sneakers, follow the method. Separate the laces from the shoes and apply a mixture of baking soda and dishwashing liquid on it. After cleaning them wipe it up with acetone and soak them for an hour or two. Bangon! White sneakers are back.

139. Use a tennis ball to remove stains of a marker from the wooden floor.

140. Roll your clothes before placing them in the suitcase. This will give you extra space to store other things as well.

141. To minimise the appearance of blemishes on your skin, take 1 tablespoon of rice flour, add half grated potato juice in it and squeeze some lemon for better consistency. Apply it all over your face and the powerful agents will work best for your skin.

142. Remove permanent marker from your home furnitures by wiping with a cloth sprayed with a hair spray.

143. Running late and forgot to brush your teeth, or ran out of toothpaste? Chew on an apple. Cinnamon sticks help as well.

144. A squeegee can be used to remove pet hair from the carpet.

145. To repel mosquitoes, use Citronella.

146. Fix your screechy wooden floors with a quick dusting of baby powder. This leaves things nice and fresh while keeping down the screeches.

147. On WornOnTV.net you can simply look up the outfit you liked in a certain TV show and buy it here.

148. Tie some Eucalyptus to the showerhead. With amazing steam bath, you can enjoy the great fragrance.

149. Mix one part of baking soda with a part of toothpaste to remove the stains of a permanent marker from a ceramic or a glass.

150. Keep small bins and baskets to store accessories and easily wrinkled clothes in the closet.

151. Rusted wrench and other hand tools? Take a pitcher of coke and dip the tools in it. Leave for some time and scrub it off.

152. Dip half a lemon in kosher salt, rub it all over the glass. Sit back and experience clear glass shower doors.

153. Remove the price slip stuck to the plastic bowl with the help of a blow dryer.

154. Remove ink stains from your favourite leather bag by dipping a cotton ball in acetone or rubbing alcohol.

155. Jar lid stuck tight? Put on a latex or rubber glove to loosen it.

156. Container smelling bed? Roll newspaper into the shape of a ball and place it inside the container. Leave for 24 hours and ta-da!

157. Get your furniture dust, hair, fur, and dirt free by wrapping duct tape around a bottle and roll it on the couches and cushions.

158. Use micellar cleansing water to clean white shoes whether it's the face of the shoe or the sole!

159. Place vanilla scented candles in a bowl of coffee beans. The warmth of the candles will heat up the beans and you will taste the aroma of french vanilla coffee in your house

160. Place vanilla scented candles in a bowl of coffee beans. The warmth of the candles will heat up the beans and you will taste the aroma of french vanilla coffee in your house.

161. For a quick touchup of your toilet use toothpaste and brush it all over. This will leave your toilet miraculously clean! (Use this occasionally :P)

162. Are your kid's toys too delicate to be tossed in the washing machine? Place them in a mesh laundry bag and select the spin cycle, clip it on a hanger and let it dry!

163. Apply acetone on your nails before applying nail paint. This will make the nail paint last longer.

164. Zip pants before laundering them. These metallic teeth can destroy other clothes being washed together.

165. Pull out the foul odour in your fridge by placing a sponge soaked in lemon juice for some hours and let it absorb the odour.

166. Fix squeaky door hinges with a cooking spray.

167. Make your eyeglasses fog free by gently rubbing a soap over them and wiping it up with a piece of cloth.

168. Clean the blades of the grinder by throwing empty egg shells and water in it. Grind it for a minute and rinse.

169. Keep your hair pins organised in a tic-tac container.

170. Use a toothbrush to get the silk threads off from a corn on the cob.

171. Clean the makeup pencil sharpeners by dipping an old toothbrush in rubbing alcohol and carefully get into the edges of the sharpener to keep it taintless.

172. Instead of cleaning the wires of the earphones with a brush use an eraserInstead of cleaning the wires of the earphones with a brush use an eraser.

Extras

1. Open an incognito tab in your browser and sign into Pandora to get unlimited skips!

2. On ShelterPups.com you can send them a picture of your dog and they'll send you a stuffed animal that looks just like it

3. When stressed by a situation(s), take a moment to think whether you will even remember this event in 5 years.

4. If you send Mickey and Minnie Mouse an invitation to your wedding they'll send you back an autographed photo and a "just married" button.

5. Clothes that are dried outside smell better because the sunlight breaks down compounds that cause any kind of odour.

6. Do a Google image search for "Atari breakout". You're welcome.

7. Set good songs as custom ringtones for people you don't like. This way, when they call you can enjoy the song while ignoring them.

8. Take some money in your wallet and put it in your winter coat. You'll have a nice surprise next year.

9. Everyone in high school be grateful that textbooks are free and hold them close to you every night and appreciate their freeness.

10. The easiest way to keep people from getting involved in your personal problems is to not post them on the internet.

11. If you ever find a drivers license you can put it in any mailbox as is and the postal service will return it to it's owner

12. Doritos are great for kindling if you can't find any.

13. If you signup on spotthestation.nasa.gov NASA will email or text you when the International Space Station is passing over your location.

14. If you send Zumiez a blank envelope they'll send it back filled with free stickers.

15. When out with friends, place your phones stacked face down in the middle of the table, first one to check their phone pays the bill! Try it!

16. You can "rewire" your brain to be happy by simply recalling 3 things you're grateful for every day for 21 days.

17. Try this! Put a finger in your ear and scratch, the sound produced is exactly the same as you are playing pacman

18. Happy and energetic people are more immune to getting colds and the flu than depressed and angry people.

19. Want to support US military? Send a soldier a care package of socks and baked goods. Those two things make a huge difference!

20. At Disney World, you can request a wake up call from any Disney character!

21. Your dance moves might not be the best, but making a fool of yourself will always be more fun than sitting on the bench alone.

22. A sick sense of humor isn't always a bad thing. People who find it easier to laugh tend to live longer than those who do not

23. A sick sense of humor isn't always a bad thing. People who find it easier to laugh tend to live longer than those who do not.

24. Never ask someone how their job search is going. It's going terribly until they tell you they got a new job.

25. Cold showers are actually good for you. They help relieve depression and help keep skin and hair Healthy & Fit.

26. Rainbow fan: Color in each fan blade a different color (red, green, blue, orange, yellow) for a cool rainbow like effect.

27. You can use toothpaste to easily remove crayon marks from walls.

28. If you're driving over 50 mph in a convertible you can theoretically put the top down and no water will get in the car. It is due to the car's windshield, which served its function as well as creating an air bubble over the interior of the car.

29. When your dog gets out, don't chase it, lie down and pretend you're hurt. They'll come back to see if you're ok.

30. Buying something from Amazon? Buy it on http://smile.amazon.com. Part of the proceeds go to a charity of your choice!

31. Prevent your pets from scratching your beloved furniture. Apply Vicks VapoRub to areas that your cat likes scratching. They usually hate the smell and will steer clear.

32. If you have to put a loved animal to sleep, find a vet who will make a house call. The animal's last hour won't be spent in a place it hates.

33. Sneak Liquor into any festival or outdoor event in a hollowed out baguette.

34. Make an autocorrect shortcut on your iphone/ipad to easily enter your email address.

35. If you fall asleep within 5 minutes of going to bed, it's an indication that you're extremely sleep deprived.

36. Cut open toilet paper rolls and use as a cuff to save your wrapping paper from unrolling.

37. 5 top foods for good skin: seafood, citrus fruits, red and green vegetables, nuts and whole grains.

38. To lose 1 pound of fat, you must run for over 3 hours. Run for 27 minutes a day, lose a pound a week.

39. If a box of candy is under 13 oz you can simply put a stamp and an address on it and it will go through the mail.

40. You are allowed to call the police if you ever see a pet alone in a hot car.

41. Life tip: Never trust a skinny cook.

42. Changing the font size of periods from 12 to 14 can make a paper look significantly longer.

43. The harder you concentrate on falling asleep, the harder it is to actually fall asleep.

44. PRANK: Buy caramel apples. Throw one away and replace it with a caramel onion!

45. Don't let yourself be controlled by three things: People, money and your past experiences.

46. Saying "Boots 'N' Cats" quickly, repeatedly and at varying tempos is the secret to beatboxing.

47. On En.Akinator.com you can think of any fictional character and it will guess it in less than 20 tries.

48. If you're walking in a bad area at night, call someone and stay on the line. If something happens, they can call the police.

49. Shoes usually become dirty very soon, there's not much we can do about that. But we can make their bottom strip white again with the help of a household cleaner!

50. You can turn an old CD spindle into a unique bagel holder.

51. At Chegg.com you can rent expensive textbooks online for a semester instead of buying them all at a bookstore.

52. Just changing the text from black to gray will make little difference to the quality of print but will not only reduce the amount of ink used, but also it'll increase the printing speed.

53. The toilet seat is the cleanest place in your house. Studies have found that on the average toilet seat there are 50 bacteria per square inch while an average cutting board have 200 times more faecal bacteria.

54. Truck drivers are always communicating with each other on the road. If you see one slow down for no reason, there's probably a cop ahead.

55. You can call the Hunger Games hotline at (404) 698-2903 and participate in the game.

56. Restaurants are required to give you free water. A good tip to know for running in the heat.

57. Out of pillow cases? Use a t-shirt.

58. The most difficult part about sewing is oftenly putting the thread through the needle. To overcome this, spray a small amount of hairspray on the end of the thread to stiffen it for easier threading.

59. Bake marbles at 325/350 for 20 min. Put in ice water to make them crack on the inside. Glue end to a necklace.

60. Microsoft holds a patent expiring in 2021, for opening a new window when you click a hyperlink.

61. If your car is ever overheating, don't keep driving it. 2 minutes of overheating is enough to completely ruin your engine.

62. Your body is actually designed to get 4 hours of sleep twice per day instead of 8 hours once!

63. Use bobby pins to get every bit out of the toothpaste tube.

64. If you lend someone $20 and you never see them again, it was worth the $20.

65. Read books In 15 minutes With Blinkist. It provides key insights from 2,000+ bestselling nonfiction books, transformed into powerful packs you can read or listen to in just 15 minutes.

66. If you hear about a party from at least three independent sources, it's going to get too big and will probably get busted.

67. If you stop and listen to a busker playing on the streets, you owe them a dollar.

68. If someone tells you a racist/sexist joke, say to them with total seriousness "I don't get it can you explain?"... Then watch them crash and burn.

69. Sex makes women's hair shinier and skin glow because of the extra oestrogen produced during the process.

70. If you ask for a puppuccino at Starbucks, they will give you a cup of whipped cream for your dog.

71. Do you always accidentally hammer your fingers? Use a clothespin to hold a nail while hammering, it will serve the purpose without harming you.

72. Put underwear and socks in shoes to save space when you go for an outing and are less on space.

73. Make your own colored smoke grenades by melting different colored crayons in a pan. Mix it with potassium nitrate, sugar and baking soda. Empty the mixture in a bottle and adjust a wick into it. Put the bottles in an empty toilet paper roll and light them up!

74. Have a bad habit of biting your nails? Always file them and have nail paint on.

75. It is a smart thought to put cup holders in the car to evade any spillage. You can connect the glass holder close to the aeration and cooling system or the armrest.

76. You can hire a professional cuddler from The Snuggery to snuggle with for $60/hour.

77. Make your own lip balm: Mix beeswax, coconut oil and shea butter in a bowl. To add some color, cut a part of your old lipstick in it and throw the bowl in a microwave for 1 minute. Take it out and put it in in an empty lid.

78. Do you possess damaged wooden furniture you want to sell? Before you go selling them, try rubbing a walnut onto the damaged areas to make it look brand new. This way you might get some extra bucks.

79. If your dog is experiencing an itchy skin, combine apple cider vinegar and green tea. Dilute it with water and clean your dog's skin twice in a day until the infection and itching are gone.

80. Clean your makeup brushes with hydrogen peroxide as an antibacterial solution added with a few drops of Castile soap or baby shampoo to a bowl of warm water.

81. On the last day of your trip to a foreign country, collect all of your loose change that will not be of any use in future and give it to the homeless.

82. It's always beneficial to get your car serviced before winter arrives. It doesn't only reduce pollution but also increases your car's life.

83. Weavers from Nimes area of France tried to replicate the Italian weaver's invention of "jeans", in the 1600's which eventually came to be known as "denim" a degradation of the words "de Nime" (from Nimes).

84. Preparing for Christmas within a small space? Instead of placing a tree, use a little tabletop vignette with candles and decorate it with some leaves!

85. Store christmas ornaments in empty egg crates to ensure their safekeeping at the end of the season and save money on purchasing container.

Food

1. Crush up Oreo cookies and put them in a salt grinder for an easy and tasty dessert toppings.

2. Buying ice cream? Press on the top of the container, if it's solid it has been properly stored, if it depresses it has thawed and refrozen.

3. Hate having bread ends? Turn the outward sides inwards to make a sandwich, perfect for little kids, they'll never know!

4. Put sprinkles on the bottom of the cone so ice cream doesn't leak out.

5. On Supercook.com you just enter what ingredients you have and it tells you what meals you can make and how you can make them.

6. Grocery stores stack their product by sell-by date, which means the oldest food's in the front. Grab the fresh food in the back!

7. Use a bread tab to hold your spot on a roll of tape.

8. Nutella + milk in the microwave will give you the best hot chocolate ever!

9. Slurping your food loudly at Japanese restaurants is actually seen as a positive gesture and indicates to the chef that you enjoy the food.

10. Put a slice of bread in a container of stale or hardened cookies to make them soft again.

11. Take a sip of coffee before adding sugar, you won't need as much sugar for it to taste as sweet afterwards.

12. Making cookies and don't have any eggs? Sure you could ask the neighbor, but half a banana (per egg) works as a good substitute!

13. Put Pancake Mix in a Ketchup bottle for a clean no-mess experience.

14. When storing empty airtight containers, throw in a pinch of salt to keep them from getting stinky.

15. Mix 1/4 cup of vinegar, honey and take 1 tablespoon 6 times a day to kill all the bacteria in your sore throat.

16. Stuff marshmallows BEFORE you roast them! Chocolate chips, peanut butter cups, strawberries... endless possibilities!

17. Turn bread upside down when cutting it, this will save it from being squished and is also easier to cut.

18. Poke a fork through the creamy part of an Oreo so you can dip the whole Oreo in milk without getting your fingers wet.

19. If no jelly is available for a PB & J, use maple syrup instead. Just as delicious.

20. To cook bacon perfectly, put it on tin foil, heat the oven to 400 degrees, and bake it for 12 minutes.

21. Caramel Apple Slices: Hollow out half an apple, pour caramel in, let harden in the freezer, cut into slices, enjoy!

22. Cauliflower dipped in barbecue sauce tastes almost the same as chicken nuggets and it's infinitely Healthy.

23. Overcooked your bacon while making breakfast? Crumble it and add it into your scrambled eggs!

24. Eating watermelon can help reduce acne breakouts and keep skin Fit and Health.

25. Honey, when mixed with vinegar and water, can remove worms and other parasites in your body.

26. If you want good running form, try to run as quietly as possible. You'll be able to run faster and longer

27. Popcorn pops better when stored in cold places like the refrigerator.

28. Replace the butter in almost every recipe with coconut oil. It has a rich, slightly sweet taste, and it's super Health & Fitness.

29. Have leftover coffee from this morning? Make coffee ice cubes. Can be used to cool iced coffee without diluting it.

30. Reheat leftover pizza on a frying pan. It'll keep the crust from getting soft.

31. Drinking chocolate milk helps relieve muscle soreness after a workout.

32. Pour pancake batter over strips of bacon to make the best pancakes ever!

33. To easily eat an orange, cut a slit in the top and the bottom and simply roll it out.

34. Freeze steak to get a perfect steakhouse crust.

35. When making tacos, put the cheese on before the meat. The cheese will melt and prevent the taco shell from breaking apart!

36. Peanut shells are edible; you don't actually have to take them off to eat the peanut.

37. Tired of the jelly soaking through your PB & J? Spread peanut butter on *both* sides of the bread and put jelly in the middle.

38. At a restaurant, you'll never go wrong ordering the chef's favorite dish.

39. When you add cream, coffee stays warm 20% longer.

40. Gatorade or Powerade is only Healthy when it's taken during a workout, and watered down. Otherwise it's all just extra sugar and empty calories.

41. To stop a popsicle from dipping on your hands, stick a muffin tin through the stick so it catches the mess.

42. Wrap your meat in cabbage to prevent the burning of meat while cooking!

43. Mixing alcohol with diet coke will get you more drunk than mixing it with regular coke.

44. Microwave a Nature Valley bar for 30 seconds to prevent crumbs when you eat it.

45. Taco hack: Wrap a soft tortilla around the crunchy one it'll hold everything way better, + you can put beans/cheese between them!

46. To reduce "onion tears," sprinkle salt on your cutting board. It will save you some te.

47. If you have just eaten a hot pepper or another spicy food, eat some yogurt. The relief comes immediately and it works better than bread or milk.

48. The easiest homemade Pizza dough: 1 cup of greek yogurt and 1 cup of self rising flour... That's it!

49. Cut your pack of bacon in half for easier baking, cleaner storage, and better size for sandwich filling.

50. Put a small amount of water in a glass when you microwave your pizza to keep the crust from getting chewy.

51. Turn your spoon upside down when pouring milk into a bowl of cereal to prevent splashing.

52. To get rid of fruit flies, fill a bowl with apple cider vinegar and a bit of soap. The vinegar attracts them, the soap will kill them.

53. Push a straw through the middle of a strawberry to easily remove the stem.

54. If you're a vegetarian, don't try and make your pets vegetarians too. It can kill them.

55. Hate that dust in the last couple bowls of cereal? Pour it into a strainer first!

56. Twist open an oreo and put in melted chocolate and a roasted marshmallow. You may call it S'moreos.

57. Eating salmon can help you grow your hair faster.

58. Extra Bacon and Extra Cheese is free of charge with the order of a Bacon Cheeseburger at Five Guys.

59. To make BLT's, or any toasty sandwich, place 2 slices of bread in a single toaster slot. This way, the bread gets toasty on the outside, but stays soft and chewy on the inside.

60. Soak your dried noodles in a bag of cold water until they become bendable then toss them into a pot of salted water at a rolling boil for one minute. This way cooked noodles will be less clumpy and less sticky.

61. The easiest way to clear a stuffy nose is to cut, peel and sniff the onion for a short period and your nose will be clear in a jiffy

62. Before you throw away a post-it, run it between the keys on your keyboard to collect crumbs and fluff.

63. Wrapping films around banana stalks slows down their ripening.

64. Honey can be adulterated easily. To test for purity, pour a small amount of honey on your thumb. If it spreads or spills easily, it might be impure.

65. Munching popcorn is great for teeth, muscle, tissues and aids digestion.

66. When washing windows, squeegee vertically outside and horizontally inside. That way if you see streaks, you'll know which side they're on.

67. Place pomegranate seeds in 'ziploc plastic bag,' snip it off from the corner and squeeze to reap the benefits of fresh pomegranate juice.

68. www.myfridgefood.com is a handy website where you put what's in your fridge and provides you bunch of recipes you can make.

69. Make sorbet by pouring a glass of juice and confining it in a baggie. Take another bag and place the juice bag into it with a bowl of ice and salt. Shake the bag till the ice turns into water. And a nice refreshing sorbet will be ready.

70. Shake a can of mixed nuts before you eat them. The larger ones will always rise to the top.

71. To stop a sneeze, use your tongue to tickle the roof of your mouth.

72. Chill onions in the freezer for 10 to 15 minutes before cutting to avoid irritation in eyes

73. Next time you go out for an Oreo shake, give it a try and make your own! Take 2 cups of vanilla ice cream, add 2 tablespoons of milk in it and put them all in a blender for 10 seconds. On the other side, take 10 Oreos and crush them up. Now, mix the blended ice cream with the crushed Oreos and guzzle on! You can also deck it with some Hershey's chocolate syrup!

74. The burn caused by eating hot peppers can only be cured with milk, and not with water, beer, or wasabi.

75. Simply touching money has been proven to reduce physical and emotional pain.

76. Nutella Cookies: 1 cup Nutella, 1 whole egg, 1 cup flour. Bake for 6-8 min at 350.

77. Amateur at cooking? Learn tips and guides on cooking at "reluctantgourmet.com."

78. Frozen water balloons can be used to keep your drinks cold enough and avoid the mess created with ice.

79. The anti-inflammatory compounds and oils found in ginger can help reduce post workout muscle soreness by upto 25 percent.

80. Hard butter? Take a glass filled with water, microwave it for 60 seconds. When done, discard the water and place the glass over the frozen butter. It will be softened after 30 seconds of removing glass.

81. Keep green onions fresh for months by chopping the remainder into small pieces and putting them in a clean, empty plastic soda bottle and place in freezer. It will preserve their flavor.

82. Toast nuts in the microwave for your morning breakfast. Preheat the microwave and leave nuts inside it for 2 minutes. Shuffle them up for an equal heating.

83. Has your recently cooked dish become a disaster with extra salt impeded in it? Here's the solution, you can use bread crumbs to nullify the effect of it

84. Slice cherry tomatoes by placing a plate over them and gliding the knife in between.

85. Lemon peel, can be used in replacement of actual zingy taste of lemon, following the steps ahead. Use your vegetable peeler to peel the skin off, avoiding the white part the (pith). Place them on the dehydrator and let them dry until they start snapping. Blend the peels and enjoy the essence of powdered lemon in your recipes.

86. Slice a lemon into pieces. Take a mason jar and fill it up with one slice of lemon and a tablespoon of sugar, repeat the process and let it infuse. Add a spoon of the mixture obtained into your morning tea!

87. Eat sushi without the rice whenever you try sushi to keep your weight under control.

88. Hard brown sugar? Put a damp paper towel on it and microwave it for 20 seconds, and Bingo!

89. To make peeling your eggs easier, place them in cold water after boiling. It helps to peel way easier.

90. Does your egg float in water? That means it is too old and isn't safe to consume.

91. Save money making espresso at home by roasting your coffee beans in an air-powered popcorn popper. Bye bye expensive Starbucks.

92. Smackdown the urge of a sweet tooth by stuffing yourself with apple and peanut butter!

93. A grapefruit knife can be used to peel the skin off of ginger.

94. Dab salt over freshly sliced apple and wash it off with water. This will not turn the slices brown after being cut for a long time.

95. Put away your usual cheese sandwich with a combination of nuts and cheese strings.

96. Peeling garlic a problem? Smash and shake garlic to separate the peels from them.

97. Litchi fruit works as a great anti oxidant. So, the next time you go on a diet, don't forget to add Litchi in your diet plan.

98. Bake eggs instead of boiling them!

99. While drinking a hot liquid, you may prevent burning your tongue by collecting saliva at the front of your tongue to insulate the sips.

100. A simple way to ensure your hard boiled eggs are super easy to peel is by adding a teaspoon of baking soda to the water while they boil.

101. Scoop out some Nutella and freeze them in the shape of discs. Take pancake mix in a bowl, add an egg, milk, and whisk them all. Place the Nutella discs on the pancake mix while cooking. Cover it with another layer and flip it off. Here you are, devouring amazing Nutella pancakes!

102. Falls fallin! It's the time for some comfy kitchen treats. Learn 3 super easy ways to make pasta in your slow Crock-Pot. Swipe up!

103. Little get-together? Grab onto your usual nachos and give them an appetizing makeover!

104. Spray apple juice on your meat before cooking as it will keep the meat juicy while you cook.

Health and Fitness

1. Deodorant on an insect bite or other itchy site will stop the itch.

2. Rub antiperspirant deodorant between your thighs to keep them from rubbing when you wear shorts.

3. Sugar can cure a burnt tongue.

4. You can heal paper cuts and immediately stop the pain by rubbing the area with chapstick.

5. Watching horror movies can burn up more than 180 calories.

6. Mosquito bite? Press a hot spoon onto the bite. The heat will destroy the chemical that caused the reaction and the itching will stop.

7. Have itchy mosquito bites? ice it, it stops the itch.

8. Cursing when in pain releases Enkephalin, which raises your pain tolerance causing you to hurt less.

9. Want to lose weight? Don't eat anything 4 hours before you go to bed. It makes a huge difference.

10. Drinking two cups of water before meals can make you lose an average of 4.5 more pounds within 12 weeks than if you don't.

11. Adding vodka to your shampoo can strengthen your hair, prevent dry scalp, and stop dandruff.

12. Ordinary/Hangover Headache Cure: Two aspirin with a bottle of Powerade. Rotate ice and heat every 15 minutes. It's a temporary method and use it only when needed occasionally.

13. Make an "X" on a bug bite with your fingernail. The itch will go away. The idea is that if you press your fingernails into a mosquito bite to make X like shape, it will spread out the toxin over a larger part of the skin to reduce the itch.

14. The two most effective treatments for battling depression are exercise and spending time with pets.

15. Fifteen straight minutes of laughter has the same Health & Fitness benefits as 30 minutes of sit-ups.

16. Showering with cooler water can stop dandruff.

17. Smoking a cigarette may interfere with your body's healing ability for nearly two weeks.

18. When you're at a restaurant, wash your hands after ordering. The menu is generally the dirtiest thing you can touch.

19. When you feel the urge to drink or smoke, go for a run, do 20 sit ups, etc. You'll start to associate quitting the habit with being fit.

20. A cure for headaches: Take a lime, cut it in half, and rub it on your forehead. The throbbing should go away.

21. A cold spoon can help remove a hickey.

22. Losing one night of sleep will impair reasoning and brain function for four days.

23. The calories in one Big Mac are equivalent to walking for 100 minutes.

24. If you're ever feeling sleepy, hold your breath as long as you can, and then breath out slowly. It increases your heart rate.

25. Want to get rid of bad breath? Brushing your teeth is important but it's more important to brush your tongue. That's where bad breath starts.

26. Drinking fruit juice doesn't even come close to the benefits of eating fruit. In fruit juice, there's often more sugar and less fiber.

27. Eating your food slowly will help you lose weight, enjoy your food, reduce stress, and lead to better digestion.

28. Eating mangoes before smoking marijuana can heighten its effects! We recommend eating mangoes alone is better :P

29. Twerking is actually good exercise! It works the deep muscles of the hips, as well as the core muscles of the lower back and abs.

30. Eating grapes improves the brain's ability to process new information and thus enhances intelligence.

31. The more organized you are, the less likely you are to develop Alzheimer's Disease.

32. A female orgasm is a powerful painkiller (because of the release of endorphins), so headaches are, in fact, a bad excuse not to have sex.

33. 9 foods that get rid of an upset stomach: Bananas, Ginger, Plain yogurt, Papaya, Applesauce, Oatmeal, White Rice, Chamomile Tea, Chicken Broth

34. Have hiccups? Hold your breath and swallow three times.

35. Have a stomach ache? Lay on your left side and rub your stomach in clockwise circles. It'll help!

36. Turn the shower to cold before you get out. It closes your pores and makes you less likely to get acne.

37. Put toothpaste(white colored) on a pimple and it will disappear over night.

38. Hate the feeling of putting cold eyedrops in your eye? Run the bottle under hot water for a few seconds, then do it. You'll barely feel em.

39. A shaving cut will immediately stop bleeding if you put Chapstick on it.

40. Exercise releases endorphins in your brain which decrease nicotine cravings.

41. Eat more marshmallows! Marshmallows relieve toothaches, asthma, sore throats, and arthritis.

42. Use parsley as a natural remedy for kidney stones by preparing its infusion in hot water and consuming multiple times a day. It contains a low percentage of sodium, which keeps a check on blood pressure and helps to prevent kidney disease.

43. If you have painful gas, lay on your back and lift your left knee to your chest. You'll fart it right out. ;)

44. Eating celery is technically exercise. When you eat celery, you burn more calories digesting it than you consume.

45. Drinking two glasses of Gatorade can relieve headache pain almost immediately, without the unpleasant side effects caused by traditional pain relievers.

46. Recipe for relaxation: exhale completely, inhale for four seconds, hold your breath for seven seconds and exhale for eight seconds.

47. Open your bag of chips from the bottom, as most of the flavor has sunk there.

48. Cuddling actually helps wounds heal faster due to the release of oxytocin.

49. The 'gel' from an Advil liquid gel will cure a pimple almost instantly.

50. A cup of coffee before a workout speeds up the fat burning process.

51. Eating breakfast in the morning makes it ten times easier to burn calories throughout the day.

52. Your sleeping style can really affect your heartburn issues. Sleeping on your left side can relieve the symptoms of heartburn.

53. The scent of bananas actually contains a compound that can help you lose weight.

54. To clear a stuffy nose easily you can push your tongue against roof of mouth, then press finger between eyebrows. Repeat 20 seconds.

55. At a Party? Tell people you're not drinking. People will start offering you a free drink!

56. The 20-20-20 rule (looking at something 20 feet away for 20 seconds every 20 min)is a method proven to stop eye strain and thus stop headaches

57. More expensive alcohols contain fewer congeners (chemicals responsible for hangovers). The more expensive the alcohol, the less hungover

58. Live in such a way that if someone spoke badly of you, nobody would believe it.

59. Eating a small amount of chocolate in the morning can help you burn calories easily and lose weight throughout the day.

60. A recent study shows that you are 47% more likely to live an extra decade if you eat home-cooked meals five times a week.

61. Be more likeable: Talk to everyone like they're your best friend, and smile a lot.

62. Onions and garlic are both foods that can accelerate hair growth.

63. Laughter and relaxation are just as vital to Health & Fitness as eating right and exercising.

64. Too much stress literally causes the human brain to freeze and shut down temporarily.

65. Sore throat? Grab a pack of JELLO but instead of putting it in the freezer, heat it up and add a teaspoon of honey. The Gelatin will coat and soothe your throat.

66. Apple Cider Vinegar will remove moles, warts and skin tags!

67. Apples are more powerful than caffeine at helping you stay awake.

68. Eat an orange before working out. Not only does it keep you hydrated, but it also prevents your muscles from getting sore.

69. Listening to music frequently will decrease your risk of a brain tumor over the course of your life.

70. Angry? Take a deep breath before you speak, because your mouth acts quicker than your brain.

71. A tablespoon of apple cider vinegar relieves allergy and asthma symptoms.

72. 30 minute naps are MOST effective because they use only 2 light sleep stages, therefore you don't wake up as tired and you are more productive.

73. Listening to music while working out can boost your running and lifting ability by almost 15%.

74. Reading a book before bed tires your eyes. As a result, your brain is tricked into feeling tired and falling asleep is easier.

75. If you laugh together for 10 minutes/day your relationship has a 75% higher chance of lasting.

76. Replace one of your meals with a healthy smoothie – frozen fruits, blend greens and coconut water or almond milk to keep yourself slim.

77. Want to lose weight? Eat more spicy food! Spicy foods fool your taste buds into being more satisfied with smaller amounts.

78. Feeling depressed? Drink water, you may be chronically dehydrated.

79. Next time you have a sore throat, eat marshmallows!

80. If you always feel like eating, you might just be dehydrated.

81. Eating plenty of unsalted sunflower seeds is a great home remedy for reducing your cholesterol level.

82. Thinking actually burns calories!

83. Moderate alcohol drinkers gain less weight over time than people who don't drink at all.

84. Eating tomatoes helps to prevent sunburn. Tomatoes provide the best defense against sun damage.

85. The keyboards at your school have statistically more germs than the toilet seats.

86. Elmer's Glue - paint on your face, allow it to dry, peel off and see the dead skin and blackheads if any. Use this only if out of resources :P

87. Drinking half a glass of water before bed and half a glass when waking up can serve as a psychological cue to remembering all of your dreams.

88. At Urnabios.com you can buy biodegradable Urns that contain a tree seed and get nutrients from your ashes. So that when you die, you can be turned into a tree!

89. The less you eat sweets, the less you crave them.

90. Life Tip: If you can't afford condoms, you can't afford kids.

91. If you're stressed, try running. Outside of meditation, it's one of the best ways to clear your mind.

92. Buy bananas in various degrees of ripeness that way, you'll have a ripe one to eat every day!

93. If you stand up too fast and you start to black out, tighten your abs as hard as you can.

94. The best way to cure hiccups is to TRY to hiccup.

95. Eating Pizza once a week can actually help reduce the risk of esophageal cancer. So go eat some Pizza!

96. Lemon juice with a pinch of salt (warm) every morning lowers cholesterol levels and brings down your weight.

97. Some McDonald's salads are actually more fattening than their burgers.

98. Drinking a tall glass of water before every meal can make you eat less and stay slim/fit.

99. Fight period cramps by mixing a few tablespoons of dry mustard in a bowl of hot water and soak your feet in it until you feel the difference.

100. When you're stressed try eating 1 cup of lowfat yogurt or 2 tablespoons of mixed nuts. The amino acids in them will help calm you down.

101. Researchers found that exposure to sleep-related words, such as "cozy," "calm," "rest," and "relax," positively affected participants' sleep.

102. Good News: You're not crazy! Hearing your name when no one is actually calling you is a sign of a healthy and fit mind.

103. Prepare a healthy "Peanut butter and blueberry waffle sandwich", for the morning. Take 2 blueberry waffles, spread peanut butter on it. Top the waffle with blueberries and cover it up with other waffle. Cut in half and serve!

104. Pickle juices are rich in vitamins and contain a decent amount of antioxidants. Grab one and start slugging!

105. Avocados boost serotonin levels. Eating them is a good way to be happy and relieve depression.

106. For every 10 years you smoke, your face ages 14 years. Tell that to someone you want to quit smoking.

107. Cook a dozen eggs at once! Put them in a muffin tin, set oven to 350 and bake for 15-20 minutes. They come out the perfect size to put on an English Muffin.

108. Pimple too painful to pop? Put it under hot water for a few seconds. This softens it and it will come off easily

109. Mineral Ice applied immediately to a burn will prevent blistering. It's cold, draws heat out and will become a brown spot that will eventually fade away.

110. Pomegranate juice can help purify blood and is an excellent cardio protective.

111. Mix oatmeal with water and spread it on the irritated skin for a soothing effect!

112. Always exercise on Monday. This sets the psychological pattern for the rest of the week.

113. Three passionate kisses a day can double your metabolic rate and can help you lose up to a pound.

114. Headache remedy drink: 3 mint leaves, 1/2 cucumber, 1/2 lemon and 1 cup filtered water.

115. Getting your hair and nails done has been proven to significantly treat anxiety and depression while also relieving stress.

116. Blowing with your thumb in your mouth can reduce your heart rate by stimulating the vagus nerve, which influences heart rate and blood pressure.

117. For a sound and peaceful sleep, place a tissue with some lavender oil sprinkled on it inside your pillowcase. This is an easy way of 'aromatherapy' at home.

118. Putting a small amount of 7UP in a flower vase will preserve them for much longer.

119. Sleeping for more than 9 hours at a time can actually damage your immune system.

120. Put one dollar in a jar as a reward whenever you complete your work-out. And in addition to good health, you will have some surplus amount stored too.

121. Consuming chamomile tea before sleeping, works the best to improve the quality of your sleep.

122. If a man takes a pregnancy test and it comes back positive, he may have testicular cancer.

123. If you're insomniac, have a glass of raw lemon juice or a spoon of honey before sleeping, this will improve your sleep!

124. While people who stay up later are likely to be more intelligent, they are also more likely to have vivid nightmares.

125. Four words to get free alcohol at a Party: I've never been drunk.

126. Stop talking about doing it and do it!

127. Black tea can help you cure nasty sunburns.

128. It is not necessary to consume protein shake after a workout. If you are drinking the shake and consuming the meal right after, you are consuming too many calories!

129. When you find yourself looking in the fridge out of boredom, drink the biggest glass of water you can find. You'll be too full to want food.

130. Any orange (also: clementine, satsuma, grapefruit, etc.) becomes easier to peel if you gently press and roll it on the table before peeling.

131. Treat herpes on your hands by adding 4-5 drops of tea tree oil in warm water. Dab a cotton ball in it and apply it to the herpes blisters.

132. One banana in the morning can help relieve

133. depression, irritable emotions, and anger.

134. Instead of grabbing a sub in the name of healthy snacking, go for tomato slices with mozzarella cheese.

135. Tell your crush you like them. You'll either get them, or you'll be set free.

136. Massage the back of your hand with ice to relieve toothache pain.

Life Tips

1. Heavens Above Fireworks is a company that turns your ashes into a firework after you die, so you can literally go out with a bang.

2. If you put your fingers in ice water immediately after painting your nails the paint will dry instantly.

3. Want kids to behave on road trips? Bring a bag of candy. Anytime they misbehave, throw a piece of candy out the window.

4. By peeing in the shower, you can save about 1,157 gallons of water a year!

5. Drinking a cold glass of water in the morning will wake you faster than a cup of coffee.

6. Lick your wrist and smell it. This is what your breath smells like to others.

7. By raising your legs slowly and lying on your back, you cannot sink into quicksand.

8. Life Tip: Don't keep all your weird shit in one drawer.

9. Put things back where you first looked for them, not where you found them.

10. If you can't afford a cab ride home, you definitely can't afford a DUI.

11. On Blahtherapy.com you can vent your problems and secrets to a total stranger.

12. Having trouble sleeping? Looking at photos of other people sleeping triggers a response in your brain that can make you feel more tired.

13. Always check your motorcycle helmet for spiders before driving down the highway doing 80.

14. After someone has a baby, stop their Facebook posts from showing up in your newsfeed. "Baby pictures flood alert

15. Boiling water before freezing it will give you crystal clear ice.

16. If you keep a condom in your wallet for longer than a month it wears down and has a 50% higher chance of breaking.

17. Your feet may be 5 to 10% larger at the end of the day than in the morning, which is why you shouldn't go shoe shopping in the morning.

18. If you're going for a run, the jog.fm app will select a music playlist for you based on your pace.

19. Life Tip: when nothing goes right, go to sleep

20. Most hotels have a huge bin of phone chargers. A good thing to know if you ever lose yours.

21. Never ever take ibuprofen to cure a hangover. On an empty stomach it can actually tear your stomach lining.

22. If you address every challenge in life under the assumption that everything always works out in the end, it usually does.

23. Tie a knot around your left earbud so you can easily tell them apart.

24. If your cat loves to sit in front of the computer, flip the top of a box upside down and set it to the side. Boxes are like magnets for cats.

25. Holding a banana peel over a bruise (for 10 to 30 minutes), will remove it's color! This technique is more of a temporary fix and not a permanent remedy.

26. If you put glow in the dark paint on your phone charger, you will never fumble in the dark again.

27. Thinking about sex will temporarily relieve the urge to pee in the case of an emergency.

28. Don't go to a restaurant 15 minutes before they close. You don't want people who hate you handling your food.

29. You are more likely to remember something you have written in blue ink than something you have written in black ink.

30. Never send your resume as a word file. Instead, print it to a PDF file, it's much cleaner and professional looking.

31. When a friend is venting to you, sometimes it's better to stay silent instead of trying to give advice.

32. Shoes too small? Put on three pairs of socks, put the shoes on, and blow dry for 10 minutes. They'll fit perfectly.

33. Whenever you're curious about something, write it down. This way, whenever you're bored you'll have an entire list of things to learn about.

34. Have a separate account on your laptop for presentations. This way, embarrassing personal things don't show up when you open it up in class.

35. Always be ten minutes early to everything. After awhile, it will become a habit and you'll never be late to anything again.

36. Good things come to those who wait & greater things come to those who get off their ass and do anything to make it happen.

37. How to get backstage at concerts and pretty much ANYWHERE: Wear a nice suit and walk quickly. People won't question you.

38. Zipper won't stay up? Flip it to the down position, it "locks" the zipper.

39. If you have to justify it to yourself and hide it from others, odds are it's a bad idea.

40. It takes 2 to 4 yrs to completely get to know someone. Couples who wait this length before marriage are less likely to get divorced!

41. The best revenge is to move on, get over it, and continue to succeed. Never give someone the satisfaction of watching you suffer.

42. If you think your life isn't interesting keep in mind that statistically you've met two future famous people.

43. When trying to find your car, keep your car remote close to your head. Your skull will actually amplify the signal range by a few car lengths.

44. If you have a tough decision flip a coin, not to decide for you, but you'll realize what you really want when it's in the air.

45. Need to remember to take something with you when you leave the house in the morning? Put it in your shoe so you can't leave without it.

46. Go 24 hours without complaining (not even once!) then watch how your life starts changing.

47. Sleeping on your right side will help you fall asleep faster than sleeping on your left.

48. Never be afraid to spend a little extra on 2 things... a bed and shoes. If you're not in one, you're in the other.

49. On camera, wearing yellow makes you look bigger and wearing green makes you look smaller.

50. While driving, move your seat as far back as you can while still being able to touch your pedals. This will help prevent speeding.

51. When someone new is hanging out with you and your friends, call your friends by their names so the new person has a chance to memorize them.

52. Try to spend more money on experiences and less on things.

53. If you need to yell at someone, you already lost the argument.

54. When meeting someone for the 1st time, ask them what they LIKE to do, rather than what they do. It'll get them excited and spark conversation.

55. You're more likely to stay focused while studying in a blue room.

56. If you have kids, remember this: the tighter the leash, the further the run when it breaks free.

57. Acne Scar Remedy: Mix a teaspoon of nutmeg and a tablespoon of honey into a paste and apply for 30 minutes. Rinse and repeat daily.

58. Tie a small piece of bright-colored fabric to your luggage. You'll be able to spot your bag in no time at the airport.

59. When a green light changes to yellow, count to four in your head. It will turn red on four.

60. Don't want to be embarrassed when buying something? Buy a birthday card with it.

61. Want to make a drink cold really fast? Wrap it in a wet paper towel and put it in the freezer for 15 minutes.

62. When a customer service representative puts you on hold they can hear everything you're saying.

63. The colder the room you're sleeping in, the more likely you are to have a bad dream.

64. You can buy fun, but you can't buy happiness. Don't get the two confused.

65. Stack your clothes vertically in your drawer to easily find your favorite shirts.

66. Get a study partner with blue eyes. Studies show that blue eyed individuals study more effectively and tend to perform better on exams.

67. Wearing headphones do not make your farts silent. Keep this in mind.

68. If your car is about to get towed, get in it. Tow trucks are forced to stop to avoid kidnapping charges!

69. Easy way to wake up: Play a game on your phone! Angry Birds, Tiny Wings, Tetris, etc. It'll stimulate your mind and get it ready for the day.

70. Wet your fingerTips and the head of the nail clippers when trimming your nails, the slices of nail won't fly off.

71. A frozen, saturated sponge in a bag makes a great icepack that won't drip all over the place when it melts.

72. If you need to get motivated, take a shower. Being clean is proven to increase your productivity.

73. If you don't like where you are, move on. You are not a tree.

74. Life Tip: Don't piss into the wind.

75. Send flowers to your wife/girlfriend anonymously. If she comes home without them, she could be cheating on you.

76. To tell if you're dreaming or not, check a clock twice. If the second time you check is drastically different from the first you're dreaming.

77. Use waxed, unflavored dental floss to cleanly slice a cake.

78. When on a date, the best way to judge a person's character is to see how they treat waiters and waitresses.

79. If a girl talks to you about a movie she wants to watch, chances are it's a hint that she wants you to ask her out.

80. The most important things in life aren't things.

81. If someone cuts you off give them the "thumbs down" instead of the middle finger. They'll think about their actions more, instead of feeling unwarranted anger towards you.

82. Hang a picture of a Tattoo you want somewhere you'll see it every day for a year. If you still want it after that, then it's worth getting.

83. Pineapple juice is 5 times more effective than cough syrup. It also prevents colds and the flu.

84. Press F2 to immediately rename a file, no more slow double clicks. (Press Enter/Return on Mac)

85. If you're ever at a Japanese restaurant, never ever rub your chopsticks together. It's a gesture that's extremely offensive to the chef

86. When filling up your car with gas, hold the trigger half way. You'll get more gas and less air in the tank.

87. The colder your room, the easier it will be to fall asleep.

88. Success isn't the key to happiness. Happiness is the key to success. If you love what you are doing, you'll be successful.

89. Behavioral scientists say that we need about 21 days to make/break a habit. So if you can go 21 days without something, you won't need it anymore.

90. Sitting on a medicine ball instead of a chair while doing work can improve your focus and productivity by 50%.

91. In college, always sit in the front of the class. You'll stand out immediately and your professor will remember you while grading.

92. If you really want something from someone, frame it as an offer rather than a request.

93. Clothes shrink too small? Soak them in a mixture of hot water and hair conditioner for 5 minutes, to unshrink them.

94. Drink tons of apple juice before you go to bed. A chemical compound in the juice will help you to have vivid awesome dreams!

95. If you ask for unsalted French Fries at McDonalds they'll make a fresh batch for you.

96. Going to a bar? Start by giving the bartender a $20 tip. You'll get amazing service the rest of the night.

97. Singing makes you happier and live longer.

98. Dropped your phone in the toilet? put it in a bag of rice. The rice will absorb the water.

99. You can be arrested for using someone's public WiFi without permission.

100. There is only one person you spend your whole life with, and that is yourself. If you aren't ok with yourself, there is an issue.

101. You can tell how much you like someone by how strong the urge is to check your phone when you're with them.

102. If you're ever homeless, spend whatever money you have on a 24 hour gym membership. You'll have a place to go at night, showers, etc.

103. Running your Bacon under cold water before cooking will reduce shrinking by up to 50%!

104. The happier you are, the less sleep you require to function in everyday life. Sadness increases the urge to sleep more.

105. Never use your favorite song as your alarm clock, you'll end up hating it.

106. Use an ice cube tray to hold small parts when disassembling and assembling things.

107. Look at someone's elbow when you High-Five. You will never miss.

108. The heavier the bottle of wine is, the better quality it is.

109. Surrounding yourself with positive people increases your life expectancy

110. If you're ever in a fight, the best spots to hit are the spots where it feels good to be massaged.

111. When you are at the pool or beach, set your flip-flops facedown. Then they won't be scalding hot from the sun when you're ready to leave.

112. Use a smaller amount of cologne. If she likes it, she'll have to get closer to you to smell it. If she doesn't, it's not overpowering.

113. When camping, strap a head light to a gallon jug of water. The tent will fill with ambient light.

114. Want someone's number at a Party? Take a picture with them and ask them to send it to you

115. In US, the Cinemark app will give you free popcorn vouchers and other rewards if you can keep your phone silent and screen dimmed during the movie.

116. Need to concentrate? Block sites for certain period of time by KeepMeOut.com and stay focused on your task.

117. Camping can cure insomnia.

118. Smiling, even in a bad mood, will immediately improve your mood. Using these muscles is enough to trigger happy chemicals in the brain.

119. Take pride in everything you do, from flipping burgers to building rockets. It will always show in the quality of your work.

120. Chew gum when you're approaching a situation that would make you nervous like public speaking or bungee jumping. If we are 'eating' something, our brain trips and it reasons 'I would not be eating if it were danger. So I'm not in danger'.

121. Trying to quit smoking? Buy the cheapest, most disgusting cigarettes you can and smoke those. It will help your willpower.

122. Rubbing Alcohol" will remove pen marks and stains from pretty much anything.

123. Get a small pan and fill with water. Add some vanilla extract and cinnamon and put on the stove. Your house will smell like a bakery.

124. Scratching the "label" side of a disc is actually more damaging to it than scratching the "underside" of one.

125. Lifting up on a door while opening or closing it will often keep it from squeaking and waking people up.

126. Call, or at a minimum, text your friends on their birthday's. Don't just give them a Facebook comment.

127. Maintain a professional-sounding email address. Nothing will turn off an employer faster than "yoloswag420@bromail.com on your job application.

128. When sharing headphones with friends, turn on mono audio on your phone to make the sound split equally.

129. If you drink more water during the day your body has less effort to do at night. This means you can get less sleep if you're well hydrated.

130. Try applying your deodorant at night instead of the morning! It'll be more effective and you'll sweat less the next day.

131. Want to cut a watermelon open without a knife? Take a quarter, make a small incision, and karate chop it in half. It seriously works!

132. Bread clips could help organize power cords easily.

133. If you're trying to quit smoking, go to a sauna 3 days in a row. You'll sweat out the nicotine and it'll be easier to quit.

134. It costs roughly $180,000 for a moderate-earning household to raise one child. It costs about $5 for a three pack of condoms. Choose wisely.

135. If everything's coming your way, you're probably in the wrong lane.

136. Going camping? Put some glow in the dark paint on your tent so you can easily navigate back to it at night.

137. Cornstarch will untangle all kinds of knots. Rub some into a knot in shoelaces, chains, string etc and watch as it comes apart

138. When going over 40 mph it is more economical to have the windows up and AC on. While under 40 mph the opposite is true.

139. Inhale through your mouth, swallow saliva twice and slowly exhale through your nose for a 100% effective hiccup cure!

140. After a job interview, if asked "Do you have any questions?" always ask "Yes, is there anything about my application that concerns you?

141. Can't brush after a meal? Gargle salt water... You'll be amazed what comes out of your mouth!

142. Don't consistently blow off your grandparents. You'll regret the time you didn't spend with them when they pass away.

143. When your kids are born, reserve them a good email address. Send them pictures, notes, etc. Give them the password on their 18th birthday.

144. Whenever you're mad at your parents just remember you vomited on them and they kept you!

145. To tell if an egg is fully cooked or raw, just spin it. If the egg wobbles then it is still raw, and if it easily spins it is fully cooked.

146. When proofreading, read out loud to yourself. Your mouth will catch errors your mind might glance over.

147. You can judge the character of a person by how they treat people who can do absolutely nothing for them.

148. The most powerful way to win an argument is by asking questions.

149. Stretch for 5 minutes before going to bed. Your muscles will be more relaxed and it'll be easier to find a comfortable position to sleep in.

150. Admit it when you're wrong and shut up when you're right. This is a simple way to drastically improve the quality of your relationships

151. Always be honest so when you have to lie, people will believe you.

152. One of the best ways to judge a person's character is to see how they treat animals.

153. Having trouble sleeping? Blink fast for a minute. Tired eyes help you to fall asleep.

154. Every 35 days your skin replaces itself. Your liver, every month. Your body make these new cells from the food you eat. So you literally are what you eat!

155. Make note of what someone does for you when you're sick. It's probably the same things that comfort them the most when they don't feel well.

156. Take a pen to your interview. Asking for a pen during an interview gives a bad impression and you'd be surprised how many people do it.

157. Life Tip: If you're going to call and say you're running late, don't walk in with Starbucks!

158. If you ever get caught sleeping on the job or in school, slowly raise your head and say "In Jesus' name, amen.

159. Feeling ugly? Go sit in Walmart for 2 hours. You will feel a lot better!

160. If someone presses all of the buttons on an elevator, you can avoid stopping on each floor by pressing each button again twice.

161. Take advantage of power outages. It's the best possible time to get a good look at the night sky.

162. Can't catch a fly? Spray it with Windex, it won't be able to fly anymore!

163. Life Tip: Never loan a friend more than you can afford to give away.

164. Never sleep naked. If there is some kind of emergency, it might be too late to put something on.

165. Exhale as much air as possible and hold to suppress laughter at inappropriate times.

166. The waiter/waitress usually has nothing to do with your food taking a long time to come. Don't punish them by not tipping if it does.

167. Safety tip: if you ever have to park in a city at night, park in front of a bank. Why? They're lit up and have cameras everywhere.

168. Cottage cheese and sour cream will last twice as long if you turn the container upside-down. This forms a vacuum and prevents bacteria.

169. When looking for a life partner; look at the level of respect a boy treats his mother, or a girl treats her father. This is the level of respect in which they will treat you in a few years.

170. Women will be more receptive to you if you compliment their abilities and skills more than their appearances.

171. No matter what you believe, if someone wishes you happy holidays, merry christmas, happy hanukkah, etc., say thank you.

172. As a general rule, any club that pats you down before you enter shouldn't be a place you should hang out at.

173. If you're the smartest person in the room, you're in the wrong room!

174. Watching the news too much has been proven to depress you and give you an unrealistic view of the world.

175. Put a sticker with a fake PIN on your debit card. If lost and someone tries to use it 3+ times, the card will be eaten.

176. Killer hangover? Try honey on crackers. The fructose in the honey will help to flush out the alcohol in your system.

177. Put a stocking over a vacuum cleaner to find tiny lost items like earrings.

178. Don't ever lie to your doctor, regardless of how embarrassed you are about something. It could save your life!

179. When you're studying/learning something new, teach a friend how to do it. Let them ask questions. If you're able to teach something well, you understand it better.

180. Windshield fogging up? Save the packets of silica beads that comes with new shoes and throw them at the side of the windshield. It wicks away any moisture.

181. Spray hairspray inside of your skirt to defend them from sticking to your legs.

182. The body oftentimes associates pain with sight. The next time you stub your toe or get a cut, look away.

183. We only need 2 close friends in whom we can trust and dedicate ourselves. Having too many friends might lead to depression and stress!

184. Accidentally text the wrong person? Immediately put your phone on airplane mode and once it fails to deliver, delete the message

185. Want to use your phone in the rain or on the beach? Put it in a ziploc bag.

186. Always go out in public dressed like you're about to meet the love of your life.

187. If you can't afford two of it, you can't afford it.

188. According to a study, smelling rubbing alcohol can relieve nausea almost instantly.

189. Keep 2 email accounts with different passwords, use one of these exclusively for registering online accounts. This will prevent a ton of spam and prevent hacking to your main account.

190. Ever had a dream where you're falling? This indicates that you have lost control of your life or have been abandoned.

191. Keep a card with all your medical info and emergency contact number in your wallet, It could save your life someday.

192. Your phone emits a radiation that's 1000 times stronger when the battery is low. Avoid answering it when this is the case.

193. Make friends with three people: a law student, a police officer, and a bartender.

194. Experiencing unwanted hair growth lately? Cut its appearance by adding 1 teaspoon of milk in 3 teaspoons of turmeric and make a thick paste. Apply in the direction of your hair growth and rinse with warm water. As the weeks will pass, the hair may become finer and would take longer to occur.

195. Do you feel groggy after a while in car even with air conditioner on? Change your car's ac to 'outside air' mode for some time. People mostly use inside air mode and end up breathing same re-circulated air.

196. Liking someone's post on a social network causes them to automatically associate you with positive thoughts. It's a worthy investment.

197. When feeling depressed, do some cleaning. Straightening out the physical aspects of your life can also bring clarity to the mental ones.

198. Adding sage to a campfire will keep insects away.

199. If someone is buying you a meal but you don't know what price-range to order in, ask them what they recommend.

200. Hair losing its shine lately? Spray some lemon juice to your hair to bring back the shine!

201. When you have to shift heavy things next time for instance books, keep them in a suitcase instead of carrying them in a carton. As they are harder to carry.

202. A person wrapped in bubble wrap will not survive a fall!

203. Yawning cools down your brain and helps get rid of stress.

204. Does your room smell bad? Tape a dryer sheet over the AC unit and turn it on.

205. Don't ask the teacher a question with 30 second of class left. People want to leave.

206. Study your notes within one day of taking them. Retention rates are 60% higher then!

207. Take an empty tissue box and attach it to a full tissue box with elastic bands. Put your used tissues in the empty box and throw it away when it's full.

208. Put old newspaper at the bottom of your trash bin, it will absorb any food juices and make for a cleaner disposal.

209. Not sure if you're in a bad neighborhood? Look at store windows. Plate glass- good. Plate glass with bars- leave before dark Plywood- leave now

210. Trouble with chopsticks? It's perfectly acceptable to eat sushi with your hands; that's the way it was originally done in Japan.

211. The best way to get someone to confess to something? Remain silent. They'll talk simply due to being uncomfortable.

212. If your toothpaste says it repairs teeth, make sure it contains "Novamin" as an active ingredient. It's the only one that actually does repair teeth.

213. Everyone talks about leaving the planet a better place for our kids. We should also leave better kids for our planet.

214. Trying hard to reach all corners of your shirt while ironing? Using a hair straightener will become your helping hand.

215. Oily hair? Here's a DIY mask you can use to rock the next hairstyle. Add 2 tablespoons of honey, 1 tablespoon of Aloe Vera gel and squeeze one lemon in the mixture. Apply it all over your hair and leave it for 20-25 minutes. After rinsing, your hair will look gorgeous and oil-free!

216. If you don't ask for it, you won't get it. You can get a lot more in life than you think simply by asking.

217. The best marriage will start as a friendship. Marrying someone you consider a close friend reduces the divorce rate by nearly 80%.

Money Savers

1. Buying a car? Buy it at the end of the month. Salespeople have quotas to meet each month and will be more likely to cut you a deal.

2. If you're the designated driver, tell the bartender. Often times they'll give you soda and/or food for free!

3. Feeling lucky? Diamondcandles.com sells candles that after so long of burning reveal a ring valuing either 10, 100, 1000 or 5000 dollars!

4. You can get a free cup of Dippin Dots on your birthday month. Just sign up for their email and they'll send you a coupon!.

5. For frequent Starbucks customers: buy and use a membership card, it only takes 5 transactions to get to the green level and then coffee and tea refills are free!

6. If you have a .edu email address, you can get an Amazon Prime account. This lets you watch almost unlimited TV/Movies.

7. Find something a Walmart you want? Make them price match it with the lowest price you can find on amazon.

8. When a price at Costco ends in $.97, it's their clearance price and that's the lowest it'll ever go

9. Cutting through aluminum foil will sharpen your knives.

10. Need some change? Put your cash into a vending machine and hit the coin return button without ordering anything.

11. Need some free WiFi? The best places to go are Panera, McDonalds, Apple Store, Office Depot, Staples, and Courtyard Marriott.

12. Each 5 mph you drive over 60 mph is like paying an additional 10 cents a gallon for gas.

13. Put a binder clip at the end of your toothpaste tube to get every last bit.

14. Want to save on your phone bill? Gmail offers free calling to anywhere in the US, as long as you have internet and a mic.

15. When you're thinking about buying something you don't necessarily need, imagine the item in one hand and the cash in the other. Which one would you take?

16. Keep a laundry basket in the back of your car to carry lots of groceries in easily.

17. You can order a "meat cube" burger from Wendy's, which consists of four patties stacked on top of each other.

18. In the US you are under no legal obligation to answer police officer's questions if you are stopped on the street.

19. When deciding to throw away clothes, ask yourself, if you were at a store would you buy it again?

20. If you want to get a new laptop, phone, or other electronic get it in October. You can usually get up to 40% off most electronics in October.

21. Want a magazine subscription but don't want to pay full price? Hit up your local library, they usually don't take out those little cards with cheaper subscriptions. Grab one!

22. Don't buy new ink cartridges, take old ones to Costco and get them filled for only $10!

23. On Halloween, any kid can get a free scary face Halloween pancake at IHOP.

24. At Shell gas stations, press the button on the side of the air pump three times. The pump will start without having to insert coins. (Worked for many people)

25. To save money, think of money as "hours of work" instead of just dollars.

26. At Chipotle, there's no limit to the number of tortillas you can order on the side.

27. Depressed? Do something really nice for someone else. It really helps!

28. If the taxi driver asks if you're "from around here," lie and say yes sometimes they drive farther (driving up the price) for tourists.

29. Put your home number in your cell phone's contact list under "Owner" that way if someone finds it they can contact you.

30. Buying a gym membership? Most times, your Health & Fitness insurance company will completely reimburse the cost for you.

31. Always go car shopping in the rain. No one wants to negotiate in the rain. The process will be quickened and most likely end in your favor.

32. Write emails to big companies and say you usually buy their product, but recently it was unsatisfactory. Free stuff will roll in!

33. You can press 1, 2, 3 etc to jump 10%, 20%, 30% into the clip you are watching on YouTube.

34. At any pickle stand in Disneyland if you ask an employee how their day was they'll give you a free pickle.

35. Never say "sorry" to another driver after a car accident. It's an admission of guilt and could be used against you in court.

36. Never buy shoes again! Payless will replace any shoes you buy from there if they fall apart or break, regardless of how long you've had them or what you've put them through.

37. Keep pen thieves away: Put a blue ink cartridge in a red pen, because no one steals a red pen!

38. AAA insurance will pick anyone up and drive them home for free on New Year's Eve.

39. Many grocery stores will sell close-to-expired foods for 50% off. Expired foods are usually still good at least a week after the date on the package.

40. When ordering coffee, ask for a medium in a large cup. They'll likely accidentally over fill it and you'll get a cheap large coffee.

41. When shopping, the cheapest items will be on the top and bottom shelves; not eye level.

42. Use condiment bottles filled with icing for an easy way to decorate cookies and cakes.

43. Out of "AA" batteries? You can use a "AAA" battery by filling the gap on the positive side with a small wad of tin foil.

44. Accidentally get deodorant on your shirt when putting it on? Rub a dryer sheet on it to take it off!

45. Wrap coupons/vouchers around the store card so you never forget them on a shopping trip.

46. Getting premium gas/petrol for a car is said to make very little difference in performance

47. To make YouTube videos load faster, right click on the video, hit settings and move the 'local storage' scroll bar all the way to the right.

48. To save some extra bucks, keep an empty plastic water bottle and refill it after passing security instead of buying overpriced water at the airport.

49. Ordering two four piece McNuggets costs less than ordering one six piece!

50. Never go to the grocery store hungry. You'll end up buying many things you don't actually need.

51. When shopping online, Google the promo codes before making a purchase. You can get anything, from free shipping to 25% off.

52. When picking a stranger to take a picture of you, make it someone you believe you can outrun. This will avoid a stolen camera.

53. Always take a look at the floor near the bar. Drunk people often drop their money!

54. Candles will burn longer and drip less if they are placed in the freezer for a few hours before using.

55. People are more likely to return a lost wallet if they find a baby picture inside of it.

56. Clear out an old lotion bottle for your beach bag and put your phone, money and keys in it for safer keeping at the beach.

57. Target will always match Amazon's price. If you find something cheap on Amazon, just buy it at Target.

58. Most car washes have a rain check policy where if it rains within 48 hours of your last visit, you can get your car washed again for free.

59. DocumentaryHeaven.com is a website that lets you watch thousands of documentaries for free.

60. If you cancel your Hulu plus trial before the 7 days are up. They'll give you the next month for free!

61. Call any pizza place and ask if they have any orders that people didn't pick up. They will let you have them at a discount price.

62. Women who walk an hour a day reduce their risk of breast cancer by upto 14%.

63. Enable private browsing whenever booking flights and hotels online. Because travel sites often track your visits and can raise the price simply because you've visited before.

64. How to navigate through a large crowd: Put pennies in a can and shake it, asking people to donate. Almost everybody will move to avoid you.

65. Is your apartment cold? Spray some water on the windows and stick bubble wrap on it. It can make you feel warmer up to 10 degrees without spending much on electricity.

66. When buying from a vending machine, insert your lowest value coin first, if the machine isn't working, you won't lose much money.

67. If "plan A" didn't work out, the alphabet has 25 more letters. Stay Cool, Calm, and Carry On!

68. Downloading the 'Honey add-on extension' to your chrome browser might help you save money by automatically applying coupons at the time of checkout.

69. Remove carpet blot with beer without spending much on bleaching and dry cleaning.

70. Get rid of rust by rubbing it with aluminum foil soaked in vinegar.

71. Instead of buying expensive cases for storing your jewelry, store your pretty petty jewelry in pill boxes.

72. As hard as it may be, establish eye contact with everyone you meet. It's one of the best ways to make people take you seriously

73. Came across a dress you probably can't take your mind off? Take a 30 days challenge and you would figure out whether it is worth buying or not.

74. Learn to prefer quality over quantity. A good pair of jean will last longer than a cheaper one.

75. Insulate storm windows in your house to reduce heat loss upto 25- 50% during inclement weather.

76. To keep potatoes from budding, place an apple in the bag with the potatoes.

77. Sweater shrink too small? Use baby shampoo to stretch it out back to normal.

78. If you have a curfew and you are a few minutes late, take a screenshot of your curfew time and show it to your parents so they think you are on time or that your clock is different. Works every time.

79. You can request a copy of the file the FBI has on you by sending them a letter.

80. You've been uploading photos on social media for long, but CoSign lets you turn them into cash. Just tag images you upload to social media with information about the products pictured in them.

Parenting

1. It is better to cut each piece of food into tiny bites with a pizza cutter instead of knife.

2. If your face latch-on issues while breastfeeding your baby, use breast shields to help the process.

3. Do your kids use walls as extended painting canvas? Well, WD-40 is the perfect crayon remover.

4. Make kids like cleaning with the 'Sweeping square game'. Google it.

5. Parents of 7 to 16 year olds can make their children behave in public by threatening to sing loudly.

6. White noise works as magic for babies. You can use some great apps from the Apple or Google Play store to make them sleep and calm.

7. Putting a medicine dropper in an open pacifier makes controlling medication less horrible.

8. Oldest siblings are smartest and youngest are the rebellious. There are some researches which prove some extent of truth behind these stereotypes.

9. . Instead of buying pricey themed cup, buy cheap ones and use stickers to avoid wastage by kiddos.

10. According to a research, older fathers have geekier sons. Now you know how long to wait :D

11. Put a marshmallow at the bottom of an ice cream cone it will stop it from dripping.

12. "Tell me more." These 3 words can intensify your relationship with your kids. Give them a chance to express and make them good orators!

13. Ever curious why do kids need so much sleep? It helps keeping their cells young.

14. Camera bags can be used as diaper bags for travelling with your kids.

15. One night it's Mom's turn to rock the cranky baby, the next day make it Dad's turn. This way mom will not be overtired.

16. Petit Pli develop clothes that grow with your kids.

17. During travel, carry duct tape. Because the moment you set that baby down in the hotel room, he will go straight for the open electricity outlets.

18. You can use toothpaste to clean permanent marker off wooden furniture.

19. To make your kids put their shoes on the correct feet, cut a sticker in half and place it on the insides of their shoes. They will always try to make sticker complete and hence put correct shoes.

20. Children notice things that you miss completely.

21. Carry an extra shirt with your baby's diaper bag, in case he/she spits in public.

22. After cutting apple slices for your child at school, tie them up together with a rubber band to keep them going brown.

23. Family vacations make a lasting impact on your child's happiness. So what are you waiting for??

24. Keep chicken nuggets warm for your children in Thermos food container with a paper towel at the bottom to absorb excessive oil.

25. If your toddler finds it hard to fall asleep, science advices to reduce the exposure to touchscreens.

26. If you are a mom of twins, make sure to feed both of them together. This will give you some time alone.

27. Mix one part Dawn dishwashing detergent into two parts hydrogen peroxide, you're amazing stain remover is ready. Bye bye poop stains :

28. Try to make your baby sleep with a little background voice. If trained to sleep in a quiet room, there are chances that they will be light sleepers and would be affected by background noises.

29. Do not spend much on buying portable beds for your kids. Instead, sew 4 pillowcases together and insert the pillows in it. They will be easier to wash and easy to drag wherever your kids go.

30. Cook desserts at home for your little ones, take a tablespoon of butter and 8 large marshmallows. Microwave for 30 seconds and add cereal rice to it. Mix them all, let it dry and enjoy!

31. Make a bracelet for your child with your phone number on it. Make them wear it whenever you go out to a crowded place.

32. You can replace the content of cola with healthy drinks like storing apple juice in it and make the kiddies chug it without force.

33. Use Pool noodles as an effective measure and prevent your toddler from hitting the corners of a coffee table.

34. Heating pads are wonderful for warming a crib mattress, it helps you transitioning your baby from sleeping in your arms to sleeping in the bed without getting him wake-up and cry.

35. Keep an organized wallet with colorful papers and pen, while your children are waiting for the food to come and crave some activity right on!

36. Don't refreeze the thawed breast milk as the milk is fit for only 24 hours to consume. Thaw as much as you need and use wisely.

37. Clean stuffed animals by coating it with baking soda and wrap it in a plastic sheet and shake well. Leave it for 15 minutes, unwrap it and brush off the baking soda.

38. Mornings are usually hectic with moms when they struggle to try new recipes for their children. Cling to this easy homemade toaster pastries to save you the time!

39. Do you have picky kids when it comes to eating veggies? Check out 4 genius ways to trick your kids to eat healthy!

Party Hacks

1. Drinking moderate amounts of alcohol before writing can actually enhance your creativity.

2. Put a glow stick in a balloon before you blow it up for night time parties.

3. Going to the beach? Put your phone in a sandwich bag and you'll still be able to use the touch screen!

4. Mountain Dew was originally made to be mixed with whiskey. Try it!

5. Soda been shaken up? Tapping the lid does nothing. Tapping the side prevents bubble buildup and soda explosion!

6. If you tend to wake up early after drinking, it might be because your blood sugar is low. A slice of bread or peanut butter can solve this.

7. Put chocolate and strawberries in an ice tray for a delicious treat.

8. Listening to music at a higher volume is proven to increase feelings of relaxation and happiness more than low volume music.

9. Want to prank your friends? Freeze Mentos in ice cubes. Serve them time bomb sodas.

10. Want to make your ice look like it came out of a fancy bar? Boiling the water removes all small particles that could prevent a clear-looking frozen cube structure.

11. How to play happy birthday on your phone. Dial:
112163
112196

11#9632
969363

12. Cut back on Oreos. A new study shows they are just as addictive as cocaine.

13. An iPhone app (BAC Alcohol Calculator) can tell you exactly how drunk you are after entering your weight and type of beverage.

14. If you're on a road trip and can't pay for a motel, park at Walmart and sleep in your car. They won't kick you out.

15. Writing an essay? Copy and paste it into Google translate and have them read it out to you. It'll be much easier to find errors this way

16. To chill bear quickly use salt with ice. Solid ice has limited points of contact with any given container, but a chilled saltwater slurry can completely surround the container and chill the bear quickly.

17. Cuddling before going to bed is 12 times more effective than sleeping pills

18. People who regularly eat fast food are nearly 51% more likely to become depressed.

19. To make Cheap Vodka bearable run it through a Brita filter couple of times and wow your guests with its improved taste.

20. Few sprigs of rosemary will make your grill smelling great - and will flavor your meat nicely as well. Your guests will surely appreciate it.

21. A handful of petroleum jelly can turn your dull looking leather shoes party ready. They might even look shinier than when you bought them.

22. When watching a DVD press stop-stop-play-skip to skip the ads and go straight to the movie.

23. Drink one glass of water for every alcoholic drink you have, you will get drunk without getting a hangover.

24. To stop yourself from vomiting, eat a mint/chew minty gum.

25. Get invited to a wedding? Set the date as a recurring event in your calendar, so you can wish them a happy anniversary every year.

26. Mix vodka + candy in a container. Wait a day, then get drunk while snacking!

27. You can order Starbucks drinks at "kids temperature" and the drink will be much cooler, saving you a burnt tongue!

28. Put your phone inside a cup/glass to amplify your party music to an appropriate volume for your party guests.

29. Cut a lemon in half, add cloves in it and place it on the table 30 minutes before placing the food. This will leave your party and food fly-free.

30. Did you just break a piece of glass? Put bread on it. The consistency of the bread will pick up even the smallest shards.

31. If you send a wedding invitation to the President in US, you might receive a congratulatory letter from him and the First Lady.

32. Put a glow stick inside each balloon before blowing up for a swanky effect after the sun goes down. It will cheer-up guests' moods.

33. Freeze fruit in ice cubes and pour them down in the water for a flavored drink!

34. Looking for good music to work to? Try game/movie soundtracks. They're designed to provide a background that won't mess with concentration.

35. When you're at a social event always hold your drink in your left hand. That way your right hand won't be cold or wet when you shake hands.

36. Put a cupcake liner over a glass bottle and insert a straw through it to keep the insects out of your guest's cocktails - and they look pretty great, too.

37. To make your ice-cream softer/easier to scoop after cooling, wrap the ice cream package in a plastic bag before putting it in the freezer. Freezer usually makes ice cream hard, wrapping helps it retain its softness.

38. Parties no longer will have to be peppy, it can be made very cozy by a bunch of readers engaging with each other and exchanging, and reading their favorite novel.

39. Break the glow stick into two and add it in a clear nail polish, apply it for a peppy look. Remember, not to swallow it.

40. Add one and a half ounces of Gin with a quarter and a half of cranberry juice. Pour a teaspoon of hibiscus lavender syrup and sparkling water. Stir them and your cocktail is ready!

41. Keep your wine chilled with frozen grapes. Unlike ice cubes, which melt in the glass, frozen grapes will not dilute the drink. They cool your wine effectively and look beautiful.

42. Ice down bottles in your washing machine to prevent the watery mess of a cooler the morning after! Simply ice down your washing machine and melting water will keep draining away.

43. Pre-scoop ice cream and store it in the freezer to save a lot of mess and time.

44. Opt for inexpensive blooms like baby's breath or carnations on your wedding. These flowers will work as fillers.

45. Spoiled carpet due to spilling of red wine? Neutralize it with white wine.

46. Labelling the names over glasses in a party can encourage the guests use the same glasses throughout the party.

47. Make a ball with aluminium foil and use it to clean the grills during the season of barbecue.

Relationship

1. If Internet Explorer can be brave enough to ask you to set him as your default browser, don't tell me you can't dare to ask a girl out.

2. If someone says "I love you" and you don't feel the same way, just say "I love YouTube" really fast.

3. Don't know what to get someone for their birthday? Have them make three guesses of "what you got them." BOOM, three things he/she wants.

4. Instead of going to dinner and a movie, go to the movie first and then dinner. This way at dinner you have something to talk about.

5. It is kinda important for you and your spouse to discuss your stands on children. This ought to be talked about before you choose to be with your partner for the rest of your life.

6. If you're friendzoned, ask to fix you up with one of her friends. She'll either feel jealous and admit her feelings or set you up on a date.

7. Do small, nice things. We assume that a big, fancy gift will strengthen our relationship but it is actually made up of hundreds of small, daily interactions, little presents and surprises.

8. DO NOT talk/ be with each other all day long. Too much of anything is bad for relationship.

9. Do not try to become your partner's 'everything'. A little space will always be appreciated.

10. It has been proven that couples who dance together are less likely to engage in emotional tensions.

11. "Would I rather be right or happy?" Always keep this question in mind in an emotionally high moment.

12. Keep that toilet seat lid down. It creates more problems in married lives than her close friends.

13. An old man once said that his wife had died and he was regretting all the time she spent cleaning instead of going out and doing things she wanted. Don't delay her plans because you need to be working in the office. You will regret it someday!

14. When she tells you her problems, don't give her advice. Just listen.

15. According to experts making one positive move triggers another from opposite side and together it creates a cascade of better interactions and lead to a better relationship. That simple huh...

16. "5-3-1" rule can help couples struggling with decision-making e.g, someone picks five possible places to eat. The other person in the relationship crosses off two options, and the one who made the initial list then crosses off another two. Problem solved!

17. While discussing your in-laws, remember that there is a specific way of doing it. Never say things like, "how could you let them do that?" it will save you lot of pain.

18. Read John Grey's 5 Love Languages. No hacks required afterwards ;)

19. Volunteer together for an activity like an environmental initiative or a programme for school kids. This makes the emotional bonding stronger than ever.

20. Holding hands while arguing, will settle things down. It is very hard to stay angry while holding hands

21. Keep writing down a note about something she liked(something to buy or a place she wanted to go) in a secret diary. Then on a special occasion get her that present. With this, she knows you care but more importantly, she knows you LISTEN.

22. For couples who are going through a huge changes in life, especially a new baby, it is extremely important to increase appreciation for one another.

23. Never argue in front of in-laws. They will always be biased. (most of the times if precise)

24. If you are expecting a fight, hold hands and go for a walk. It's extremely difficult to get angry while holding hands

25. Physical intimacy isn't just about sex. Cuddling and holding hands are way more cute!

26. If your other half is an avid reader, you can simply get a 'YES' with a little effort. Cut out some pieces from a book (probably not one of their favourite ones) and place a ring in it. And let's hope your streak of luck begins!

27. Keep revealing your flaws to the people you want to be close to, becoz this will make you more relatable to them.

28. If you ran out of gift ideas for your other half, buy them an electric blanket this Christmas!

29. Gifts are the coal in love fire. Buy something useful instead of swanky like get her a sketchbook if she's got the talent but doesn't do anything about it or a guitar if he ever discussed his love for it.

30. Read 'Kierkegaard' concept of love and after all these centuries, he will sort your love life up.

31. Always remember frequent smaller acts of kindness greatly trump large rare acts of kindness.

32. Do similar things. Recommend books, TV shows, music, movies, news and etc. Reading, watching and listening to the same things will give you topics in common to talk.

33. Choose a week during which, once a day, you will do one surprising, positive thing for your mate. Start by singing his/her favourite song or making him/her breakfast. Will boost the romance like crazy.

34. Extremely New Relationship: be honest, starting a relationship on lies is something you will regret later. Unharmful and cute lies might be allowed if you tell the truth shortly after.

35. Ask a girl about that one thing or animal she is most afraid of. Try your best to make her fearless!

36. Every time you intend to disagree, argue, or correct your loved one, ask yourself: is this actually something i care about?

37. 80% of women use silence to express pain and anger. If she has started ignoring you, there are a hell lot of chances that she is hurt.

38. Don't argue about things you don't care about, most of the times we fight for things that are purely insignificant for us. Keep your love before your egos for lasting relationship.

39. Nascent Stage Relationship: Compliment him/her, tell her something that no one would tell. It will set you apart from all of her friends. Never overdo the compliments.

40. Define acceptable perimeters on social media. Like 'can having a private chat is acceptable if your partner is there?' If you answer no, you know what should not be done.

41. Make yourself happy and then allow your spouse to increase your happiness. A person who can't be happy by its own drains the good mood out of a room.

42. A key to building closeness within a marriage is if you can't handle his/her friends/habits/likeness then befriend them. It is one of the most prominent reason for divorce.

43. Send each other postcards or hand-written love letters sometime. It's one of the cutest thing to do.

44. Beloved's birthday approaching? Buy him/her a pair of a wireless beanie with inbuilt headphones. Buy one from Amazon.

45. Saying I love you is still the best phrase to keep it warm!

46. Do something your partner is interested in, and you aren't. Tough but works like a charm!

47. Prove yourself wrong sometimes.

48. Exhibiting your skills in a non-bragging way will interest your partner. She will notice and unfold your talent gradually.

49. Use a silly codeword or phrase to pacify an argument. Make a pact that you will stop arguing and hug each other whenever that codeword is being said in an argument.

50. Try to co-blog! Think about various topics and collaborate with each other on it. This will enhance your productivity and will add up to your relationship!

51. According to studies, it takes three years to truly know the person you're with. Don't rush into something.

52. Create something creative together. Be anything: a small craft, a creative meal, an event or anything.

53. A tried and tested way to keep the spark alive and get over gloomy periods is to do something out of the ordinary. Challenge your boy for a race or a game on sunday afternoon. Thank us later ;)

54. Show your love for your other half in all senses. Appeal the 5 senses of smell, taste, sight, touch, and sound and prepare things to let them experience each one of it with you!

55. Apologize only when you really feel it in your heart, that it is your fault, instead of doing it for the sake of ending the quarrel and move ahead.

56. 90% of the text messages are read within 3 minutes of their delivery. So, the next time your girlfriend gets angry, you know exactly where to send those cheesy texts!

57. Trying to win her heart? Ask her questions about all the guys who tried to persuade her with all those cheesy lines. Both of you would die laughing and as a brownie point, she will state of all those things she is tired of hearing.

58. Focusing too much on the bad builds resentment. Instead, focus on the good things like the way he always brings you coffee in the morning. It will make you appreciate your partner and find more joy in relationship.

59. Hide chocolate at random places in house. When girlfriend is in distress and calls you to complain about feeling terrible, tell her to look under the couch cushion, behind the plant, etc.

Study Boosters

1. mathway.com solves all kinds of Math homework problems with step-by-step explanations.

2. Drawing diagram helps you better memorize it.

3. Laminate your notes, so that the tears may roll off before exams :P

4. Now open your eyes and find your project/question paper and say "Now i'm ready for next 40 minutes.

5. Keep your sticky notes organized by pasting different sized post-it notes in a notebook with a hot glue. And, never lose them again!

6. Chewing gum is actually a brain booster. It's not backed by any concrete research but scientists think it's based on the act of chewing keeps us awake and focused.

7. While listening to long hours of lecture, turn on instrumental music in background with very mild sound. It will help you focus through long boring session.

8. Study in a group only if everyone has read the study material. You do not gain much if this is not the case.

9. Googling 'site:edu [subject] exam,' helps you to find exam papers on the same topic

10. Stick to paper! 90% students have agreed that hard copies tend to leave an indelible imprint on our mind.

11. While studying, take a short review at every 25 minute interval of the newly learned topic to prevent skimming.

12. Keep yourself motivated by plotting a graph on a paper demonstrating number of problems you solved.

13. Listen classical music while study. Not knowing the lyrics of a song means brain doesn't split its focus.

14. habitica.com - game that improves good habits.

15. Write down all the formulas at the very beginning of the exam, you are prone to forgetting them in pressure as the time passes.

16. Finding troubles with maths problem? Put the equation into WolframAlpha.com and it will solve for you.

17. Spotify has a great collection of music for concentrating better. Just search 'Study' and keep reading!

18. Using different colours while taking notes can break the monotony while reading them.

19. Instrumental music and unfamiliar songs will help you to concentrate better rather than listening to your favorite music which can turn out to be negative for your productivity.

20. Rewriting notes by hand is a good habit to learn more effectively than using gadgets.

21. After studying things, ask yourself the relevancy of the topic and what did you learn from it. This will increase your critical analysis.

22. Become a learned student as well as a benefactor of the society by visiting 'freerice.com.' On it, you can answer questions based to test vocabulary. For every right answer, the World Food Programme will donate 10 grains of rice to fight hunger.

23. Want to survive your back to back finals? Keep an orange along with you. Brazilian studies show that the refreshing smell of the fruit will make you feel less anxious.

24. Get into an uncomfortable area while studying because you are most likely to sleep if you get cozy with your bed and blanket.

25. Improve your brain's functioning by indulging in certain exercises like reading, solving puzzles or playing music. More work you let your brain do increases its ability to memorize concepts.

26. Keep your brain stimulated by going to your old school practices of doodling and sketching. It boosts your brainpower and improves concentration.

27. Times new roman is the fastest font to read.

28. You're more likely to retain information from your class if you review what you've learned every day. As simple as it sounds.

29. Use "Chunking" to learn anything. People remember things better if learn related ideas in small chunks.

30. Watching documentaries on a relevant topic is an entertaining method of grasping a whole set of knowledge in a quick. History topics are best suited for this method.

31. On 'poemhunter.com', you can find any poem from the 1,333,561 poems from classical poets, themes, new poets and popular all at one platform.

32. Want to complete your homework without being interrupted by someone? Put your headphones, even if you're not listening to any music.

33. You are more likely to improve the quality of your study notes if you try and imagine you're making them for someone else.

34. Develop your own word sequences to remember things easily e.g, BODMAS and BBROYGBVGW.

35. Make a cheat sheet. Though you'll obviously never use it during an actual exam, but in order to do so, you'll need to go through all of your notes to find the most important parts and rewrite them on your sheet.

36. Find articles on trending topics and stay updated with random stuff at "Snopes.com."

37. Studying at a green surrounding or glancing at colour green can make you more creative.

38. Stick important bits of information like formulas, equations etc. you need to remember on fridge door, somewhere near your bed or at any places that you look at often.

39. Create flowcharts and diagrams for school projects, business on "Lucidchart." Export your files and diagrams in form of a PDF and sync it absolutely anywhere.

40. Close your eyes and imagine that situation where you had an academic success. Congratulate yourself for doing the fantastic work.

41. talktyper.com converts speech to text, in case you want to cut short the time to write.

42. First drafts are meant to be imperfect. Keep going!

43. Speaking out loud instead of simply reading increases your chances of remembering by 50%.

44. 20 minutes exercise before an exam can improve performance.

Survival

1. Life Tip: Buy a fire extinguisher before you need a fire extinguisher!

2. If you're outside in the woods and cut yourself, spiderwebs can not only seal the wound but also make it heal much faster. But do not attempt to make your own spider web bandage when you live in a place full of poisonous spiders.

3. Any working cell phone, regardless if it is in service or not, will call 911.

4. If you're ever drunk and need to sleep in your car, take the keys out of the ignition. It's a DUI if they are still in there.

5. The Calvin Klein "Obsession" scent should never be used when going into the woods. It attracts cheetahs, tigers and jaguars.

6. If you suspect someone's checking you out, yawn. If they yawn back, they were (yawning is visually contagious!).

7. Don't put your feet up on a car's dashboard. Airbags go off like small bombs and it can easily break both of your legs.

8. Get something in your eye? Fill a bowl of water big enough for your face & open your eyes in it. It'll come right out.

9. Exhale when your left foot hits the ground to avoid cramps while running.

10. If you're swimming towards the shore and find yourself moving out, you're caught in a riptide. You must swim parallel to the shore to escape it.

11. If you get pulled over at night turn on your interior light. It helps ease the officer by showing you have nothing to hide.

12. If there is ever a Zombie apocalypse go to Costco. Large cement walls, an endless supply of food, and you have to have a costco card to get in.

13. If you're about to get hit by a car (and can't jump sideways), jump UP! It'll give you a better chance of rolling over the car.

14. If you are in for a long drive at night, listen to comedians while driving. It's impossible to fall asleep while laughing

15. If you ever get kidnapped and they tie your hands together and put tape over your mouth, lick the tape until it falls off.

16. Put a dab of honey over a zit and cover with a band-aid overnight. When you wake up, the zit will be gone with no scar.

17. Never feed bread to ducks. They can't digest it properly and it could kill them.

18. Bees can't see you if you aren't moving.

19. In the woods with no edible resources other than mushrooms it's lucrative to try them but avoid bright coloured mushrooms, as most of them are poisonous.

20. If you get buried under snow by an avalanche, spit and saliva will follow gravity. Dig the opposite way.

21. The National Suicide Hotline number: 1-800-784-2433. It can be accessed 24/7. Call anytime.

22. As soon as you have brain freeze, push your tongue against the roof of your mouth, it will instantly relieve the pain.

23. You can use an acorn cap as a whistle if you ever get lost in wild. Getting lost from your group can be frightening, so it's nice to know you can use your surroundings to help you.

24. Apply toothpaste to burns, it soothes the pain and stops the burning.

25. If you ever get trapped underwater in your car, use your carseat headrest to break the window.

26. Thirsty at a remote place? LifeStraw cleans water you normally couldn't drink.

27. You can make soda can tabs into hooks for fishing with the help of scissor.

28. If you're coughing uncontrollably, raise your hands above your head and it will stop!

29. Before going on a wild trek get guides to the most common edible plants. It will make a difference between life and death if you get stuck there.

30. 6 movies to watch to learn survival. Dawn of the Dead, San Andreas, The Day after Tomorrow, Zombieland, The Edge and Into the Wild.

31. Falling air pressure causes pain in bird's ears, so if birds are flying low to the ground it almost always means a thunderstorm is coming.

32. If you ever suspect someone is following your car, take four right turns. It forms a circle, and if they're still behind they're following.

33. Sitting in the back of a plane makes you 40% more likely to survive a crash.

34. Ever wonder a way to avoid crying when chopping onions? Keeping onions cold reduces vapour formation and reduces its effect on eyes. Cutting under a running tap also works fine.

35. If you live in the northern hemisphere the moss grown on trees will be far more prevalent on the side of the tree that is pointing south. Use this in case GPS or mobile is dead.

36. To escape from a crocodile's jaws, push your thumbs in its eyeballs, it will let you go instantly.

37. When you call 911 in US, the FIRST thing you should give them is your location. They immediately send police when they have an address.

38. Every November 7th is "bring your own cup day" at 7/11.

39. A foil-backed gum/candy wrapper can be used to start a fire if you have a battery source e.g., from a flashlight or remote. Simultaneously touch the positive and negative terminals of the battery with the foil side of the wrapper.

40. Make waterproof matches by dipping the first half of the matchstick in clear nail polish. Dry, and then dip the other half to seal it. Make sure to stay away from glittery polishes.

41. Breathe quickly before going underwater to hold your breath longer.

42. Set a stick into the ground. Mark the end of the shadow from the stick. This tip will be west. Wait for at least fifteen minutes and notice that the tip have moved. The imaginary line between the two will be your East to West.

43. When people are angry at you, if you stay calm it'll get them even angrier, and be ashamed about it after.

44. Chips can be used as fire starters as they burn easily and can be used in wild scenarios.

45. In a case of emergency, you can use crayon colours as candles. They can burn for 30 minutes.

46. Polypore mushrooms can give you an enormous advantage if you need to start a fire, or carry a smoldering ember from one place to another. They have hard, almost woody caps that may have a smooth or rough texture.

47. Don't put your hands in the pocket while coming down from stairs. If you slightly dis-balance you wouldn't be able to hold on.

48. Don't stand in the doorway during an earthquake. They are not stronger than any other place in your house. Get under a table or corner instead.

49. If you are afraid of the frost bite, baby oil can be your savior!

Technology

1. If your phone battery is really low and you need it for later don't turn it off. Instead, put it on airplane mode. Turning it off and on will waste more battery life.

2. On AccountKiller.com you can instantly remove all of your personal data from websites you don't want having it.

3. On windows search "size:gigantic" and it will display all files on your computer >128mb. Use this to clean up space on your hard drive.

4. If you have a computer that blocks sites such as YouTube, Google Chrome's incognito mode will let you access them.

5. The "HolaUnblocker" extension on Google Chrome will allow you to access to UK version of Netflix; thus unlocking many more shows and movies.

6. When letting someone use your iPhone to call someone, use Siri from the lock screen. They can call, but not look at texts/photos etc.

7. Need to focus on studying? Screen Time is an app that lets you limit the time you use on your iphone or ipad. Set the time, press start and when it expires it closes whatever you were doing.

8. If you play YouTube videos through Safari you can still listen to them with your phone's screen turned off.

9. Replace the "en" in a Wikipedia link with "simple" to strip away the complex and mostly irrelevant information on the page.

10. Accidentally erase something you just typed on your iPhone? To undo that, just shake it!

11. When filming video at a concert using your phone, put a finger over your phone's microphone. It'll sound clearer when you play it back.

12. On SnesFun.com you can play almost every single old Nintendo game!

13. Starbucks offers a size smaller than Tall: Short! Cheaper, and a much Healthy size. Just ask the barista.

14. For the best sound in a movie theater, sit 2/3 of the way back and as close to the middle as possible; this is where the audio engineer sits when they do the final mix.

15. To get explicit tracks on iTunes Radio: play any station, click the "I" in the top center and turn explicit tracks on.

16. On Televisor.com you can enter a show you like and it will recommend new shows to watch and where to find them online.

17. To resize a photo for Instagram, tilt your phone sideways and take a screenshot of it. It'll fit perfectly without affecting the quality.

18. You can search "[month] [year]" in Wikipedia to give you all the major world news for that month.

19. Always use the custom installation option when installing software. This will show you exactly what you're downloading and prevent you from installing unwanted toolbars, software, etc.

20. Remove negative people from your life. The people you spend time with influence your attitude, thoughts and success more than you think.

21. White wine will take out a red wine stain.

22. If you have many different online accounts, NameChk.com you can see every website where your username has been used

23. Fronto is an Android app that displays ads on your lock screen, this means you get paid every time you unlock your phone.

24. Wanna write essays and bibliographies like a PRO: Get the info from Wikipedia, and cite the sources listed at the bottom.

25. If you type "Google gravity" and then hit "I'm feeling lucky" on Google the entire page will lose its gravity and you can play with it.

26. The Easybib iPhone app will give you a bibliography on any book if you simply scan the barcode.

27. Refreshing Pandora will change the song without using any of your skips.

28. If you type in any flight number into Google you can see exactly where the plane is.

29. To move frame by frame on Youtube, pause the video and then use J or L to go backward or forward respectively.

30. Drop a battery from 6 inches off the ground, if they give one small bounce and fall over they're good. If they bounce around anymore they're dead or almost dead.

31. If you download a "PDF" file and you see it ends in "exe" delete it. It's usually a virus.

32. Drinking helps fight against Radioactive Poisoning.

33. Your headphones can be used as microphones if you plug them into the mic jack on your computer. This is helpful when recording lectures.

34. If you lost an Android phone in your house and it's on vibrate, you can find it by going to Google Play>Android device manager>'Ring'

35. If you need to get a gift for a girl, check out her Pinterest account. You'll find ideas within seconds.

36. If your smartphone or tablet ever gets slow, clean the touch screen with an eye glass wipe to get the dirt and oils off.

37. Forgot your computer password? Boot up in safe mode (F8 during startup), login as administrator and then change your password.

38. Sign up for the free 30 minute trial of on-board WiFi while flying. Delete cookies when trial ends. Start new trial.

39. To listen to a song on Youtube on repeat without having to keep pressing 'replay' at the end, add 'repeat' between 'www.Youtube' and '.com'.

40. 10minutemail.com gives you a fake email address so you don't have to use your own personal email address when signing up for things.

41. Swipe left or right on the iPhone calculator to delete the last digit. You won't have to start all over.

42. Hit alt and click on and any google image to have it automatically saved to your computer.

43. Laughing for 15 minutes has the same Health & Fitness benefits as getting two extra hours of sleep.

44. By saving an Excel file as an .XLSB you can shrink the size by half or 75%

45. While typing in MS Word, delete a single word at a time by simply using CTRL+ Backspace

46. Start doodling on autodraw.com and "AutoDraw" will start suggesting a better version of your art!

47. If your phone freezes, plug it into a charger. This might free it up again.

48. Contrary to popular belief-thinking of the future is usually what keeps people up at night; thinking of the past can actually help you sleep.

49. Save your PowerPoint presentation as a "PowerPoint Show" (.ppsx) and it will open directly to the slideshow.

50. To re-open an accidentally closed browser tab, use Ctrl/Cmd + Shift + T.

51. Is your roommate a sleepy head? Probably, then their habit of snoozing up the alarm must be annoying. To acquire some peace and sleep there, you can call up the offending phone and hang up when the phone starts ringing.

52. Use www.youtube.com/leanback to find youtube trends.

53. ProxTube allows you to watch regionally blocked YouTube videos

54. Walking in a scary area at night? Download a police scanner app for your phone and listen to it on full volume

55. Take aesthetic shots for Instagram on VSCOcam.

56. The most humble way to accept a compliment is to say "thank you", not to tell the other person that they're wrong.

57. Download and use a Mobile Virtual Network (VPN) app. It allows you to connect to an abroad server, and to use apps that are not available in your country.

58. You can learn Spanish, French, Italian, German and Portuguese for free on Duolingo.com

59. At www.archive.org/web you can see archived versions of websites from year ago. It is also called "waybackmachine".

60. Want to download a YouTube video as an mp3? Put "listento" after the "www." in the URL.

61. If you type "do a barrel roll" into your Google search, the whole page will spin. Try it!

62. Play MP3, youtube videos directly on chrome browser by dragging files in chrome window.

63. Many-a-times, you can extend the length of a free trial by pushing back the date on your computer.

64. If you ask Siri to read a text for you and the text has Emojis she will give you a description of the Emoji for you.

65. You can use your windows calculator for EMI calculations also. Follow calculator-view-worksheets-Mortgage

66. You can search articles based on your location by hitting, http://en.wikipedia.org/wiki/Special:Nearby no matter on which place you are visiting.

67. Your laptop battery can last longer if you charge it up to only 80% instead of the full 100%. The fact is linked to heating of laptop on higher percentage which reduces battery life.

68. Command+shift+3 takes a screenshot on MacBooks.

69. Search 'Find My Phone' In Google and you may locate your phone easily if the phone is connected to internet. You may also lock your phone or erase all the data easily.

70. Save hard to remember yet important information at your mouse click without leaving the browser by adding a chrome extension of "Permanent clipboard."

71. You can create a GIF out of YouTube videos by adding Gif before YouTube in url.

72. Fond of watching Disney animated tales ? 'cornel1801/disney/movies.html' gives you a free access and nostalgia at the same time!

73. www.noisli.com generates background noise to keep you focused and improve your creativity.

74. Hitting the Spacebar will scroll you down a web page; hitting the Spacebar + Shift lets you scroll back up.

75. Find fascinating articles on varied topics of mental health, decision making, books and much more on " www.farnamstreetblog.com."

76. Make better looking presentations on "Canva." Once you are done, download the pdf and convert the file into a ppt.

77. The voice recorder does not only fulfills the requirement of quirky voice notes you share. Instead, it can be used to record the lectures where the teacher is a marathoner.

78. To quickly change the case (upper vs. lower) of text in Microsoft Word, highlight the phrase, then hit Shift + F3.

79. Save videos from facebook on your android device with an installation of an app: "MyVideoDownloader for Facebook."

80. www.discuvver.com is a website that redirects you to a random useful website everytime you click.

81. Got fond of that new track and tired of playing it manually again? Follow this immediate trick : Play it on 'youtubeloop.net' and get high on!

82. Need to write a quick note while browsing internet? Open a temporary notepad in your browser by typing "data:text/html, <html contenteditable>" into the search bar.

83. multcloud.com, allows you an integration among various cloud storage platforms and gives an easy access to have them at a single spot.

84. Want to use your own handwriting as a font? Visit "calligraphr.com" and create your own font.

85. Let your Iphone tell you who is calling by customizing the vibrations. You can create different buzzes: in Contacts, select the person of your choice and hit Edit. In it you will find numerable vibrations and can also create your own!

86. Win + W — opens Windows Ink Workspace (notes, screenshots). Mostly goes unnoticed.

87. Bored? Just google, 'Google in 1998.' And go back to basics!

88. Your hunger for a good movie can be restored by simply visiting AGoodMovieToWatch.com and hunt down a good movie for the upcoming weekend.

89. Is your browser safe against tracking? Check it on "Panopticlick."

90. If you forgot the title of a song but remember the melody or lyrics to it, hum/sing it on Midomi.com to get the song title.

91. WhatsApp allows you to create shortcut for your favourite contact. Open the contact/group and follow: click on top right menu > click 'More' >click 'Add shortcut' and the shortcut will be created on your home screen.

92. With 'Snapchat', you can zoom in to read any information from quite a far, better than your usual camera. P.S - The quality shall not remain the best.

93. With 'Pushbullet.com,' you can sync your mobile phone with your computer and the notifications will pop on your computer screen.

94. A heated laptop can be cooled down with placing forks underneath it

95. HowLongToReadThis.com helps you to test your reading speed per minute and how long will you take to complete your next read.

96. WhatsApp allows you to create and share GIFs easily. Open the contact and follow: Click on attach icon > select gallery and choose a video > In the edit activity, adjust video length to up to 6 seconds > slide to GIF option and you are ready.

97. Want astounding edited pictures on your phone with just some swipes? Use Camera ZOOM FX- FREE, and try Holga 35mm. It gives a perfect look to your pictures as if captured by a professional camera.

98. Want to save your phone battery? Use dark wallpaper or theme

99. Long tiring essays and articles scare you? You can now summarize the articles by using the chrome extension TDLR. It gives you the nuts and bolts of a long article in a single click

100. An app- Duolingo, teaches you numerous languages for free!

Made in the USA
Middletown, DE
26 November 2020